German
Vocabulary

BROCKHAMPTON
PRESS

This edition published 1995 by Brockhampton Press, a
member of Hodder Headline PLC.

ISBN 1 86019 047 2

Printed and bound in Slovenia.

Contents

The Body   *Der Körper*

1

head	der Kopf
hair	das Haar, die Haare *pl*
dark	dunkel
fair	hell
bald	glatzköpfig
brown (hair)	braun
smooth	glatt
curly	gelockt
grey hair	graue Haare *pl*
scalp	die Kopfhaut

2

face	das Gesicht
features	die Mine
forehead	die Stirn
cheek	die Wange
wrinkle	die Falte
dimple	das Grübchen
chin	das Kinn
beautiful	schön
handsome	gut aussehend
pretty	hübsch

3

ugly	häßlich
ugliness	die Häßlichkeit
beauty	die Schönheit
beauty spot	der Schönheitsflecken
freckle	die Sommersprosse
freckled	sommersprossig
ear	das Ohr
hearing	das Gehör

to hear	hören
listen	zuhören

4

listener	der Zuhörer
earlobe	das Ohrläppchen
deaf	taub
mute	stumm
deaf-mute	taubstumm
deafness	die Taubheit
to deafen	betäuben
deafening	ohrenbetäubend
eardrum	das Trommelfell
sound	der Ton

5

noise	der Lärm
eye	das Auge
sense	der Sinn
eyesight	der Gesichtssinn
tear	die Träne
eyebrow	die Augenbraue
to frown	die Stirn runzeln
eyelid	das Augenlid
eyelash	die Wimper
pupil	die Pupille

6

retina	die Netzhaut
iris	die Iris
glance	der flüchtige Blick
to see	sehen
to look	schauen
look	der Blick
visible	sichtbar
invisible	unsichtbar

blind	blind
blindness	Blindheit

7

to blind	blenden, blind machen
blind spot	der tote Winkel
one-eyed	einäugig
cross-eyed	schielend
to observe	beobachten
to notice	bemerken
expression	der Ausdruck
to smile	lächeln
smile	das Lächeln
to laugh	lachen

8

laugh	das Lachen
laughing *adj*	lachend
mouth	der Mund
tongue	die Zunge
lip	die Lippe
tooth	der Zahn
eyetooth	der Eckzahn
gum	das Zahnfleisch
palate	der Gaumen
to say	sagen

9

saying	der Ausdruck
to speak	sprechen
to shout	schreien
to be quiet	schweigen
touch (sense)	der Tastsinn
to touch	berühren
to feel	fühlen
tactile	taktil, tastend

nose	die Nase
nostril	das Nasenloch

10

bridge (nose)	der Nasenrücken
smell (sense)	der Geruchssinn
smell	der Geruch
to smell (of)	riechen (nach)
to taste (of)	schmecken (nach)
to taste	schmecken, probieren
taste (sense)	der Geschmack
taste bud	die Geschmacksknospe
tasty	schmackhaft
tasting	die Probe

11

moustache	der Schnurrbart
beard	der Bart
facial hair	die Gesichtsbehaarung
sideburns	der Backenbart
dandruff	die Schuppen *pl*
plait	der Zopf
curl	die Locke
to shave	sich rasieren
to grow a beard	sich einen Bart stehen lassen
bearded	bärtig

12

clean-shaven	rasiert
jaw	der Kiefer
throat	die Kehle, der Hals
neck	der Hals
shoulder	die Schulter
back	der Rücken
chest	der Brustkasten
breast	die Brust

| to breathe | atmen |
| breath | der Atem |

13

breathing	die Atmung
lung	die Lunge
windpipe	die Luftröhre
heart	das Herz
heartbeat	der Herzschlag
rib	die Rippe
side	die Seite
limb	das Glied, die Gliedmaßen *pl*
leg	das Bein
lame	gehbehindert

14

to limp	hinken
thigh	der Oberschenkel
calf	der Unterschenkel
tendon	die Sehne
groin	die Leistengegend
muscle	der Muskel
knee	das Knie
kneecap	die Kniescheibe
to kneel	knien
foot	der Fuß

15

heel	die Ferse
toe	die Zehe
sole	die Sohle
ankle	das Fußgelenk
instep	der Spann
arm	der Arm
forearm	der Vorderarm
right-handed	rechtshändig

left-handed	rechtshändig
right	rechts

16

left	links
hand	die Hand
to handle	hantieren
handshake	das Händeschütteln
handful	die Handvoll
finger	der Finger
index finger	der Zeigefinger
thumb	der Daumen
palm	die Handfläche
nail	der Nagel

17

wrist	das Handgelenk
elbow	der Ellbogen
fist	die Faust
knuckle	der Knöchel
bone	der Knochen
spine	das Rückgrat
dorsal skeleton	das Skelett
skull	der Schädel
blood	das Blut
vein	die Vene

18

artery	die Arterie
capillary	das Blutgefäß
liver	die Leber
skin	die Haut
pore	die Pore
sweat	der Schweiß
to sweat	schwitzen
scar	die Narbe

wart	die Warze
complexion	der Teint

19

brain	das Gehirn
kidney	die Niere
bladder	die Blase
spleen	die Milz
gland	die Drüse
larynx	der Kehlkopf
ligament	das Band
cartilage	der Knorpel
womb	der Mutterleib
ovary	der Eileiter

20

height	die Größe
big	groß, dick
small	klein
tall	groß
short	klein
fat	dick
thin	dünn
strong	stark
strength	die Stärke
weak	schwach

21

knock-kneed	mit X-Beinen
bow-legged	mit O-Beinen
to stand	stehen
to stand up	aufstehen
to raise	heben
to lie down	sich hinlegen
to sleep	schlafen
sleep	der Schlaf

to be sleepy	müde sein
to dream	träume

22

to doze	vor sich hindösen
to fall asleep	einschlafen
asleep	schlafend
to be awake	wach sein
to wake up	aufwachen
drowsy	schläfrig
dream	der Traum
nightmare	der Alptraum
conscious	bei Bewußtsein
unconscious	bewußtlos

Clothes — *Die Kleider*

23

jacket	die Jacke
trousers	die Hose *sing*
jeans	die Jeans *pl*
dungarees	die Latzhose *sing*
overalls	das Overall
braces	die Hosenträger *pl*
sweater	der Pullover
sock	die Socke
to darn	stopfen
raincoat	der Regenmantel

24

overcoat	der Mantel
to shelter	bergen
to protect	schützen
hat	der Hut
brim	der Rand

shadow	der Schatten
cap	die Kappe, Mütze
glasses	die Brille
earmuffs	die Ohrenwärmer
walking stick	der Gehstock

25

umbrella	der Regenschirm
cloth	der Stoff
fine	fein
thick	dick
coarse	grob
shirt	das Hemd
T-shirt	das T-Shirt
tie	die Krawatte
handkerchief	das Taschentuch
suit (men)	der Anzug
suit (women)	das Kostüm

26

waistcoat	die Weste
skirt	der Rock
miniskirt	der Minirock
blouse	die Bluse
stockings	die (langen) Strümpfe *pl*
veil	der Schleier
beret	die Baskenmütze
collar	der Kragen
gloves	die Handschuhe *pl*
belt	der Gürtel

27

scarf	der Schal
handkerchief	das Taschentuch
button	der Knopf
to button	zuknöpfen

to unbutton	aufknöpfen
new	neu
second-hand	aus zweiter Hand
graceful	anmutig
narrow	eng
broad	breit

28

ready-made	fertig, Konfektion
to make	machen
to get made	machen lassen
to wear	tragen
to use	verwenden
worn out	abgetragen
useful	nützlich
useless	nutzlos
practical	praktisch

29

housecoat	das Hauskleid
nightdress	das Nachthemd
pyjamas	der Schlafanzug
underpants, knickers	die Unterhose *sing*
petticoat	der Unterrock
slip	das Unterkleid
bra	der Büstenhalter
leotard	der Gymnastikanzug

30

coat hanger	der Kleiderbügel
zip	der Reißverschluß
wristband	die Manschette
sweatshirt	das Sweatshirt
shorts	die kurze Hose *sing*, die Shorts *pl*
tracksuit	der Jogginganzug
dress	das Kleid

to dress	kleiden
to dress oneself	sich anziehen
to take off	ausziehen

31

to remove	entfernen
to undress	sich ausziehen
naked	nackt
to put	aufsetzen
to put on	anziehen
sash	die Schärpe
apron	die Schürze
shawl	der Schal
sleeve	der Ärmel
to sew	nähen

32

seam	der Saum
seamstress	die Näherin
thread	der Faden
needle	die Nadel
hole	das Loch
scissors	die Schere
ribbon	das Band
linen	das Leinen
lace	die Spitze
velcro	der Klettverschluß

33

fur	der Pelz
furry	aus Pelz
silk	die Seide
silky	seidig
velvet	der Samt
cotton	die Baumwolle
nylon	der Nylon

fan	der Fächer
in fashion	modisch
out of fashion	unmodern

34

dressmaker	der Schneider, die Schneiderin
pocket	die Hosentasche, die Rockta-sche
bag	die Tasche
pin	die Stecknadel
to tie	zubinden
to untie	aufmachen
to loosen	lösen
sandal	die Sandale
slipper	der Hausschuh
pair	das Paar

35

lace	der Schnürriemen
shoe	der Schuh
sole	die Sohle
heel	der Absatz
to polish	putzen
shoe polish	die Schuhcreme
shoehorn	der Schuhlöffel
boot	der Stiefel
leather	das Leder
rubber	der Gummi

36

suede	das Wildleder
barefoot	barfuß
to put on one's shoes	sich die Schuhe anziehen
to take off one's shoes	sich die Schuhe ausziehen
footwear	die Fußmoden *pl*
shoemaker	der Schuhmacher

ring	der Ring
diamond	der Diamant
necklace	das Halsband
bracelet	das Armband

Family and Relationships
Familie und Beziehungen

37

father	der Vater
mother	die Mutter
parents	die Eltern *pl*
son	der Sohn
daughter	die Tochter
children	die Kinder *pl*
brother	der Bruder
sister	die Schwester
brotherhood	die Brüderschaft
brotherly	brüderlich

38

elder	älter
younger	jünger
husband	der Ehemann
wife	die Ehefrau
uncle	der Onkel
aunt	die Tante
nephew	der Neffe
niece	die Nichte
grandfather	der Großvater
grandmother	die Großmutter

39

grandparents	die Großeltern
grandson	der Enkel

granddaughter	die Enkelin
boy	der Junge
girl	das Mädchen
cousin (male)	der Cousin, der Vetter
cousin (female)	die Cousine, die Base
twin	der Zwilling
baby	das Baby, der Säugling
child	das Kind
to be born	geboren werden

40

to grow up	aufwachsen
name	der Name
surname	der Nachname
birthday	der Geburtstag
age	das Alter
old	alt
to get old	alt werden
old man	der alte Mann
old woman	die alte Frau
youth	die Jugend

41

young	jung
young man	der junge Mann
young woman	die junge Frau
father-in-law	der Schwiegervater
mother-in-law	die Schwiegermutter
son-in-law	der Schwiegerson
daughter-in-law	die Schwiegertochter
brother-in-law	der Schwager
sister-in-law	die Schwägern
orphan	der Waise, die Waise

42

stepfather	der Stiefvater

stepmother	die Stiefmutter
stepson	der Stiefsohn
stepdaughter	die Stieftocher
stepbrother	der Stiefbruder
stepsister	die Stiefschwester
bachelor	der ledige Mann
spinster	die ledige Frau
widower	der Witwer
widow	die Witwe

43

ancestor	der Vorfahre
descendant	der Nachkomme
boyfriend	der Freund
girlfriend	die Freundin
couple	das Paar
love	die Liebe
to fall in love	sich verlieben
to marry	heiraten
wedding	die Hochzeit
honeymoon	die Flitterwochen

44

maternity	die Mutterschaft
paternity	die Vaterschaft
to be pregnant	schwanger sein
to give birth	gebähren
childbirth	die Geburt
nurse	die Amme
child minder	das Kindermädchen
to baby-sit	babysitten
baby-sitter	der Babysitter
godmother	die Patin

45

godfather	der Pate

baptism	die Taufe
to baptise	taufen
creche	das Kinderbett
to breastfeed	stillen
infancy	die frühe Kindheit
to spoil (child)	verderben
spoiled	verdorben
divorce	die Scheidung
separation	die Trennung

46

family planning	die Familienplanung
contraception	die Empfängnisverhütung
contraceptive	das Verhütungsmittel
contraceptive pill	die Anti-Baby-Pille
condom	das Kondom
abortion	die Abtreibung
to have an abortion	abtreiben lassen
period	die Periode, die Regel
to menstruate	menstruieren
to conceive	schwanger werden

47

middle-aged	mittleren Alters
menopause	die Wechseljahre *pl*
to retire	in den Ruhestand gehen
pensioner	der Rentner, die Rentnerin
the aging process	der Alterungsprozeß
old age	das Alter
death	der Tod
to die	sterben
dying	sterbend
deathbed	das Totenbett

48

dead man	der Tote

dead woman	die Tote
death certificate	die Sterbeurkunde
mourning	die Trauer
burial	die Beerdigung
to bury	beerdigen
grave	das Grab
cemetery	der Friedhof
wake	die Totenwache
coffin	der Sarg

49

deceased, late	verstorben
to console	trösten
to weep	weinen
to wear mourning	Schwarz tragen
to survive	überleben
survivor	der Überlebende, die Überlebende
crematorium	das Krematorium
cremation	die Einäscherung
to cremate	einäschern
ashes	die Asche *sing*

Health   *Die Gesundheit*

50

sickness	die Krankheit
nurse	die Krankenschwester, der Krankenbruder
infirmary	das Krankenhaus
sick	krank
hospital	das Krankenhaus
patient	der Patient, die Patientin
cough	der Husten
to cough	husten

to injure	verletzen
injury	die Verletzung

51

cramp	der Krampf
to cut oneself	sich schneiden
to dislocate	ausrenken
faint	schwach
to be ill	krank sein
to become ill	krank werden
to look after	sorgen für
care	die Sorge
careful	sorgsam

52

carelessness	die Sorglosigkeit
careless	sorglos
negligent	nachlässig
doctor	der Arzt, die Ärztin
medicine	die Medizin
prescription	das Rezept
pharmacist	der Apotheker, die Apotheker
pharmacy	die Apotheke
cure	die Heilung
curable	heilbar

53

incurable	unheilbar
to cure	heilen
to get well	gesund werden
healthy	gesund
unhealthy	ungesund
to recover	sich erholen
pain	der Schmerz
painful	schmerzhaft
to suffer	leiden

54

diet	die Diät
obesity	die Fettleibigkeit
obese	fettleibig
anorexic	magersüchtig
anorexia	die Magersucht
obsession	die Besessenheit
to get fat	dick werden
headache	der Kopfschmerz
aspirin	das Aspirin
migraine	die Migräne

55

toothache	der Zahnschmerz
stomach upset	die Magenverstimmung
indigestion	die Verdauungsstörung
food poisoning	die Lebensmittelvergiftung
sore throat	der Halsschmerz
hoarse	heiser
pale	blaß
to turn pale	erblassen
to faint	ohnmächtig werden
cold (illness)	die Erkältung

56

to catch a cold	sich erkälten
wound	die Wunde
surgeon	der Chirurg
to heat	heizen
hot	heiß
temperature	die Temperatur
perspiration	der Schweiß, das Schwitzen
sweaty	verschwitzt
fever	das Fieber
germ	der Keim

57

microbe	die Mikrobe
contagious	ansteckend
vaccine	der Impfstoff
to shiver	zittern
madness	die Verrücktheit
mad	verrückt
drug	die Droge
pill	die Pille
to scar	vernarben
stitches	die Stiche

58

to relieve	lindern
swollen	geschwollen
boil	der Furunkel
to bleed	bluten
to clot	ein Gerinnsel bilden
blood cell	die Blutzelle
blood group	die Blutgruppe
blood pressure	der Blutdruck
blood test	die Blutuntersuchung
check up	der Test

59

epidemic	die Epidemie
plague	die Pest
allergy	die Allergie
allergic	allergisch
angina	die Angina
tonsillitis	die Mandelentzündung
fracture	der Bruch
cast	der Gips
crutches	die Krücken
wheelchair	der Rollstuhl

60

haemophiliac	der Bluter
haemophilia	die Bluterkrankheit
cholesterol	das Cholesterin
vitamin	das Vitamin
calorie	die Kalorie
handicapped person	der Behinderte, die Behinderte
handicap	die Behinderung
pneumonia	die Lungenentzündugn
heart attack	der Herzanfall
bypass operation	die Bypass-Operation

61

heart surgery	die Operation am Herzen
microsurgery	die Mikrochirurgie
pacemaker	der Herzschrittmacher
heart transplant	die Herztransplantation
smallpox	die schwarzen Pocken *pl*
stroke	der Schlaganfall
tumour	der Tumor
HIV positive	HIV-postiv
AIDS	(das) AIDS
cancer	der Krebs

62

breast cancer	der Brustkrebs
chemotherapy	die Chemotherapie
screening	die Reihenuntersuchung
diagnosis	die Diagnose
antibody	der Antikörper
antibiotic	das Antibiotikum
depression	die Depression
depressed	depressiv
to depress	deprimieren
to undergo an operation	sich operieren lassen

63

painkiller	das Schmerzmittel
treatment	die Behandlung
anaesthetic	die Narkose
anaesthetist	der Narkosearzt, die Narkose- ärztin
donor	der Spender, die Spenderin
genetic engineering	die Genmanipulation
test-tube baby	das Baby aus dem Reagenzglas
surrogate mother	die Leihmutter
infertile	unfruchtbar
hormone	das Hormon

64

psychologist	der Psychologe, die Psychologin
psychology	die Psychologie
psychoanalyst	der Psychoanalytiker, die Psychoanalytikerin
psychoanalysis	die Psychoanalyse
psychosomatic	psychosomatisch
hypochondriac	der Hypochonder
plastic surgery	die plastische Chirurgie
face-lift	das Lifting
implant	das Implantat
self-esteem	das Selbstbewußtsein

65

to smoke	rauchen
passive smoking	das passive Rauchen
to inhale	inhalieren
withdrawal syndrome	die Entzugserscheinung
alcohol	der Alkohol
hangover	der Kater
alcoholic	der Alkoholiker, die Alkoholike- rin

drug addict	der Drogenabhängige
drug addiction	die Drogenabhängigkeit
drugs traffic	der Drogenhandel

66

heroin	das Heroin
cocaine	das Kokain
drugs trafficker	der Drogenhändler
to launder money	Geld waschen
syringe	die Spritze
to inject	injizieren
to take drugs	Drogen nehmen
clinic	die Klinik
outpatient	der Patient in ambulanter Behandlung
therapy	die Behandlung

Nature   *Die Natur*

67

world	die Welt
natural	natürlich
creation	die Schöpfung
the Big Bang theory	die Big-Bang-Theorie
supernatural	übernatürlich
to create	schaffen
sky	der Himmel
galaxy	die Galaxie
the Milky Way	die Milchstraße
the Plough	der große Wagen, der große Bär

68

astronomer	der Astronom, der Sternenkundige
astronomy	die Astronomie
telescope	das Teleskop

UFO	das UFO (unbekannte Flugobjekt)
light year	das Lichtjahr
asteroid	der Asteroid
meteor	der Meteorit
comet	der Komet
star	der Stern
starry	sternenübersäht

69

to twinkle	funkeln
to shine	leuchten
planet	der Planet
earth	die Erde
Mercury	der Merkur
Venus	die Venus
Mars	der Mars
Jupiter	der Jupiter
Saturn	der Saturn
Neptune	der Neptun

70

Uranus	der Uranus
Pluto	der Pluto
orbit	die Umlaufbahn
to orbit	umkreisen
gravity	die Schwerkraft
satellite	der Satellit
moon	der Mond
eclipse	die Sonnenfinsternis
sun	die Sonne
sunspot	der Sonnenflecken

71

ray	der Strahl
to radiate	strahlen

radiant	strahlend
to shine	leuchten
shining	leuchtend
brilliancy	die Leuchtkraft
sunrise	der Sonnenaufgang
to rise	aufgehen
sunset	der Sonnenuntergang
to set (sun)	untergehen

72

dawn	die Morgendämmerung
dusk	die Abenddämmerung
to grow dark	dunkel werden
earthquake	das Erdbeben
volcano	der Vulkan
eruption	der Ausbruch
deserted	verlassen
desert	die Wüste
plain	die Ebene

73

flat	flach
level	eben
valley	das Tal
hill	der Hügel, der Berg
mountain	der Berg
mountainous	bergig
peak	die Spitze, der Gipfel
summit	der Gipfel
range of mountains	die Bergkette
crag	die Felsspitze

74

rock	der Felsen
steep	steil
slope	der Abhang

coast	die Küste
coastal	Küsten-
shore	das Ufer
beach	der Strand
cliff	das Kliff
sea	die See, das Meer
tides	die Gezeiten *pl*

75
high tide	die Flut
low tide	die Ebbe
ebb tide	die Ebbe
flood tide	die Flut
wave	die Welle
foam	die Gischt
tempest	der Sturm
hurricane	der Hurrikan
gulf	der Meerbusen
bay	die Bucht

76
cape	das Kap
straits	die Meerenge *sing*
island	die Insel
spring,	die Quelle
fountain	die Quelle
waterfall	der Wasserfall
stream	das Flüßchen
river	der Fluß
current	die Strömung
draught	der Luftzug

77
glacier	der Gletscher
iceberg	der Eisberg
ice cap	die Eiskappe

icefloe	die Eisscholle
to flood	überfluten
flood	die Flut
border	die Grenze
lake	der See
pond	der Teich
marsh	das Marschland

78
deep	tief
depth	die Tiefe
weather	das Wetter
fine, fair	schön
climate	das Klima
barometer	das Barometer
thermometer	das Thermometer
degree	der Grad
air	die Luft
breeze	die Brise

79
cool, fresh	kühl, frisch
wind	der Wind
windy	windig
dampness	die Feuchtigkeit
damp	feucht
to wet	befeuchten
wet	naß
storm	der Sturm
stormy	stürmig
dry	trocken

80
drought	die Trockenheit
to dry	austrocknen
rainbow	der Regenbogen

rain	der Regen
rainy	regnerisch
to rain	regnen
drop	der Tropfen
shower	der Schauer
cloud	die Wolke
cloudy	wolkig

81

to cloud over	sich bewölken
to clear up	sich aufklären
lightning	der Blitz
lightning conductor	der Blitzableiter
to flash (lightning)	blitzen
sheet lightning	der Flächenblitz
fork lightning	der gegabelte Blitz
harmful	schädlich
to harm	schaden
thunder	der Donner

82

to thunder	donnern
fog	der Nebel
mist	der Dunst, der Nebelschleier
foggy	neblig
misty	dunstig
snow	der Schnee
to snow	schneien
snowstorm	der Schneesturm
snowfall	der Schneefall
hailstone	der Hagel

83

to hail	hageln
to freeze	frieren
frozen	gefroren

icicle	der Eiszapfen
frost	der Frost
to thaw	tauen
ice	das Eis
thaw	das Tauwetter
heatwave	die Hitzewelle
sultry	schwül

Minerals — *Minerale*

84	
metal	das Metall
mine	die Mine
forge	die Schmiede, das Hüttenwerk
to forge	schmieden
steel	das Stahl
iron	das Eisen
iron *adj*	eisern
bronze	die Bronze
brass	das Messing
85	
copper	das Kupfer
tin	das Zinn
lead	das Blei
zinc	das Zink
nickel	das Nickel
aluminium	das Aluminium
silver	das Silber
gold	das Gold
platinum	das Platin
mould	die Form
86	
to extract	gewinnen
to exploit	abbauen

miner	der Grubenarbeiter
to melt, smelt	schmelzen
to mould	formen
rust	der Rost
rusty	rostig
to solder	schweißen
to alloy	legieren
alloy	die Legierung

87

stone	der Stein
stony	steinig
quarry	der Steinbruch
granite	der Granit
to polish	polieren
polished	poliert
smooth	glatt
marble	der Marmmor
lime	der Kalk
chalk	die Kreide

88

clay	der Ton
sulphur	der Schwefel
jewel	der Edelstein
pearl	die Perle
diamond	der Diamant
ruby	der Rubin
emerald	der Smaragd
mother-of-pearl	der Perlmutt
enamel	das Email
sapphire	der Saphir

89

agate	der Agat
opal	der Opal

lapis-lazuli	der Lapislazuli
obsidian	der Obsidian
garnet	der Granat
alkali	das Alkali
acid	die Säure
acidity	der Säuregrad
plutonium	das Plutonium
radium	das Radium

Animals   *Tiere*

90

domestic animal	das Haustier
tame	zahm
cat	die Katze
kitten	das Kätzchen
to mew	miauen
feline	zur Familie der Katzen gehörend
claw	die Klaue
dog	der Hund
bitch	die Hündin
puppy	die Welpe

91

to bark	bellen
canine	zur Familie der Hunde gehörend
watchful	wachsam
watchdog	der Wachhund
guardian	der Wächter
pet	das Haustier
breed	die Rasse
greyhound	der Windhund
alsatian	der Schäferhund
terrapin	die Dosenschildkröte
tropical fish	die tropischen Fische *pl*

92

aquarium	Aquarium
aquatic horse	Seepferdchen
to neigh	wiehern
stallion	der Hengst
mare	die Stute
colt	das Fohlen
donkey	der Esel
to bray	iahen
mule	der Maulesel

93

male	das männliche Tier
female	das weibliche Tier
livestock	der Tierbestand
horn	das Horn, das Geweih
paw	die Pfote
hoof	das Huf
tail	der Schwanz
flock	die Herde
cow	die Kuh
ox	der Ochse

94

to low	muhen
bull	der Stier
calf	das Kalb
heifer	die Jungkuh
lamb	das Lamm
sheep	das Schaf
sheepdog	der Schäferhund
ram	der Widder
ewe	das Mutterschaf
goat	die Ziege
pig	das Schwein

95

to grunt	grunzen
to fatten	mästen
wild, savage	wild
carnivorous	fleischfressend
herbivorous	pflanzenfressend
omnivorous	allesfressend
quadruped	der Vierbeiner
biped	der Zweibeiner
mammal	das Säugetier
warm-blooded	warmblütig

96

predator	das Raubtier
prey	die Beute
lion	der Löwe
lioness	die Löwin
cub	das Löwenjunge
to roar	brüllen
mane	die Mähne
tiger	der Tiger
tigress	die Tigerin
cheetah	der Cheetah

97

leopard	der Leopard
lynx	der Luchs
mountain lion	der Berglöwe
hyena	die Hyäne
jackal	der Schakal
scavenger	der Aasfresser
to scavenge	Aas fressen
carrion	das Aas
jaguar	der Jaguar
tapir	der Tapir

98

buffalo	der Büffel
mongoose	der Mungo
porcupine	das Stachelschwein
armadillo	das Gürteltiel
skunk	das Stinktier
sloth	das Faultier
rhinoceros	das Nashorn
hippopotamus	das Nilpferd, Flußpferd
wolf	der Wolf
pack	das Rudel

99

bear	der Bär
to hibernate	überwintern
zebra	das Zebra
stripe (of the zebra)	der Streifen
bison	das Bison
to graze	grasen
pasture	die Weide
wild boar	das (männliche) Wildschwein
ferocious	wild
bristle	brüchig

100

elephant	der Elefant
trunk	der Rüssel
camel	das Kamel
hump	der Höcker
dromedary	das Dromedar
llama	das Lama
deer	das Wild
doe	das Reh
stag	der Hirsch
elk	der Elch

101

moose	der Amerikanische Elch
hare	Geweih
fox	der Fuchs
cunning	schlau
craft, cunning	die Schlauheit
hare	der Feldhase
badger	der Dachs
otter	der Otter
dormouse	die Haselmaus
shrew	die Spitzmaus

102

hedgehog	der Igel
weasel	das Wiesel
mink	der Nerz
mink coat	der Nerzmantel
beaver	der Biber
dam	der Damm
mole	der Maulwurf
molehill	der Maulwurfhügel
mouse	die Maus
mousetrap	die Mausefalle

103

rabbit	das Kaninchen
(rabbit) hutch	der (Kaninchen)stall
rat	die Ratte
bat	die Fledermaus
nocturnal	Nacht-
primates	die Menschenaffen *pl*
gorilla	der Gorilla
monkey	das Äffchen
orang-utan	der Orang Utan
baboon	der Pavian

104

gibbon	der Gibbon
marsupial	das Beuteltier
kangaroo	das Känguruh
koala	der Koalabär
giant panda	der Riesenpanda
invertebrate	wirbellos
exoskeleton	Außenskelett
insect	das Insekt
to hum	summen
humming	das Summen

105

antenna	der Fühler
worm	der Wurm
to worm	sich schlängeln
earthworm	der Regenwurm
tapeworm	der Bandwurm
parasite	der Parasit
beetle	der Käfer
stag beetle	der Hirschkäfer
silkworm	der Seidenwurm
caterpillar	die Raupe

106

chrysalis	die Puppe
metamorphosis	die Verpuppung
to metamorphose	sich verpuppen
butterfly	der Schmetterling
moth	die Motte, der Nachtfalter
fly	die Fliege
bluebottle	die Schmeißfliege
spider	die Spinne
web	das Netz
to spin	spinnen

107

wasp	die Wespe
hornet	die Hornisse
to sting	stechen
sting	der Stich
bee	die Biene
worker (bee, ant)	die Arbeiterin
bumblebee	die Hummel
queen bee	die Bienenkönigin
beehive	der Bienenstock
apiary	das Bienenhaus

108

apiarist	der Bienenzüchter
drone	die Drone
honey	der Honig
honeycomb	die Bienenwabe
grasshopper	der Grashüpfer
locust	die Heuschrecke
to infest	befallen
cricket	die Grille
glow-worm	das Glühwürmchen
ant	die Ameise

109

anthill	der Ameisenhügel
colony	die Kolonie
to itch	jucken
itch	der Juckreiz
termite	die Termit
troublesome	lästig
to molest	belästigen
mosquito	die Stechmücke
net	das Netz
malaria	die Malaria

110

flea	der Floh
earwig	der Ohrwurm
praying mantis	die Gottesanbeterin
scorpion	der Skorpion
snail	die Hausschnecke
slug	die Nacktschnecke
louse	die Laus
lousy	verlaust
centipede	der Tausendfüßler
millipede	der Tausendfüßler, die Landassel

111

reptile	das Reptil
cold-blooded animal	der Kaltblüter
tortoise	die Landschildkröte
turtle	die Wasserschildkröte
crocodile	das Krokodil
alligator	der Alligator
serpent	die Giftschlange
snake	die Schlange
slowworm	die Blindschleiche
harmless	harmlos

112

crawl	kriechen
viper	die Viper
fang	der Giftzahn
python	die Python
anaconda	die Anakonda
rattlesnake	die Klapperschlange
cobra	die Kobra
poison	das Gift
antidote	das Antidot
poisonous	giftig

113

bird	der Vogel
aviary	das Vogelhaus
ostrich	der Strauß
beak, bill	der Schnabel
wing	der Flügel
to fly	fliegen
flight	der Flug
flightless	flugunfähig
to lay (eggs)	(Eier) legen
to nest	nisten

114

budgerigar, budgie	der Wellensittich
canary	der Kanarienvogel
robin redbreast	das Rotkehlchen
chaffinch	der Buchfink
nightingale	die Nachtigall
sparrow	der Spatz
swallow	die Schwalbe
lark	die Lerche
cuckoo	der Kuckuck
magpie	die Elster

115

blackbird	die Amsel
crow	die Krähe
to caw	krächzen
seagull	die Möve
albatross	der Albatros
cormorant	der Kormoran
partridge	das Rebhuhn
pheasant	der Fasan
stork	der Storch
owl	die Eule

116

rooster	der Hahn
cockcrow	der Hahnenschrei
to crow	krähen
cock-a-doodle-do	kikeriki
hen	das Huhn, die Henne
feather	die Feder
to pluck	rupfen
chicken	das Hühnchen
to brood	brüten
to breed	züchten

117

pigeon	die Taube
duck	die Ente
goose	die Gans
swan	der Schwan
parrot	der Papagei
toucan	der Tukan
turkey	der Truthahn
peacock	der Pfau
hummingbird	der Kolibri
bird of paradise	der Paradiesvogel

118

rapacious	gefräßig
bird of prey	der Raubvogel
eagle	der Adler
vulture	der Geier
peregrine falcon	der Wanderfalke
to swoop	sich herabstürzen
hawk	der Habicht
to hover (hawk)	schweben
falcon	der Falke
condor	der Kondor

119

amphibious	amphibisch
amphibians	die Amphibien *pl only*
frog	der Frosch
bullfrog	der Ochsenfrosch
tadpole	die Kaulquappe
toad	die Kröte
salamander	der Salamander
crustacean	das Krustentier
crab	der Krebs
prawn	die (Stein-)Garnele

120

fish	der Fisch
goldfish	der Goldfisch
piranha	der Piranha
voracious	gefräßig
carp	der Karpfen
sturgeon	der Stör
caviar	der Kaviar
trout	die Forelle
hake	der Hecht
herring	der Hering

121

sardine	die Sardine
skate	der Glattrochen
cod	der Kabeljau
eel	der Aal
electric eel	der Zitteraal
elver	der Jungaal
salmon	der Lachs
tuna fish	der Thunfisch
school (of fish)	der Schwarm
coral reef	das Korallenriff

122

flipper, fin	die Flosse
gills	die Kiemen *pl*
shell	die Schale
seashell	die Muschel
scale	die Schuppe
squid	der Kalmar
octopus	der Oktopus
tentacle	der Fangarm
cuttlefish	der Tintenfisch
crayfish	der Flußkrebs

123

lobster	der Hummer
sea urchin	der Seeigel
sea horse	das Seepferdchen
starfish	der Seestern
shellfish	das Schalentier
oyster	die Auster
shark	der Hai
whale	der Wal
killer whale	der Mörderwal
dolphin	der Delphin

124

seal	der Seehund
sea lion	der Seelöwe
walrus	das Walroß
natural selection	die natürliche Auswahl
survival of the fittest	die natürliche Zuchtwahl
evolution	die Evolution
to evolve	sich entwickeln
zoology	die Zoologie
zoologist	der Zoologe
zoo	der Zoo, der Tiergarten

125

habitat	der Lebensraum
extinct	ausgestorben
dinosaur	der Dinosaurier
mammoth	der Mammut
dodo	die Dronte
yeti	der Yeti
mythical	sagenhaft, sagenumwoben
myth	die Sage, der Mythos
unicorn	das Einhorn
dragon	der Drache

Plants   *Die Pflanzen*

126

to plant	pflanzen
to transplant	umpflanzen
root	die Wurzel
to root (pig, etc)	schnüffeln nach
to take root	Wurzeln schlagen
to uproot	entwurzeln
radical	radikal
tendril	die Ranke
stalk	der Stiel
sap	der Saft

127

foliage	das Laub
leaf	das Blatt
leafy	belaubt
to shed leaves	die Blätter verlieren
deciduous	Laub-, jährlich die Blätter abwerfend
evergreen	Immergrün-
perennial	mehrjährig

thorn	der Dorn
thorn tree	der Dornenbusch
thorny	dornig

128

weed	das Unkraut
to weed	Unkraut jäten
to thin	ausdünnen
thistle	die Distel
nettle	die Brennessel
briar	die Heckenrose
hemlock	der Schierling
deadly nightshade	die Tollkirsche
Venus flytrap	die Venus-Fliegenfalle
rush	die Binse

129

reed	das Schilf
epiphyte	die Schmarotzerpflanze
moss	das Moos
spider plant	die Tradescantie
bud	die Knospe
to bud	Knospen treiben
flower	die Blume
to flower	blühen
blooming	blühend
petal	das Blütenblatt

130

to wither	verdorren
withered	verdorrt
garland	die Girlande
scent	der Duft
garden	der Garten
gardener	der Gärtner
to water	bewässern

watering can	die Gießkanne
irrigation	die Bewässerung

131

herb	das Kraut
thyme	der Thymian
rosemary	der Rosmarin
sage	der Salbei
parsley	die Petersilie
mint	die Minze
tarragon	der Estragon
coriander	der Koriander
dill	der Dill
watercress	die Brunnenkresse

132

balsam	das Rührmichnichtan
chicory	der Chicorée
chives	der Schnittlauch
mustard	der Senf
balm	die Melisse
clover	der Klee
grass	das Gras
shrub	der Strauch
myrtle	die Heidelbeerre
gorse	der (Stech-)Ginster

133

flowerbed	das Blumenbeet
pansy	das Stiefmütterchen
primrose	die Primel
daisy	das Gänseblümchen
anemone	die Anemone
tulip	die Tulpe
hyacinth	die Hyazinthe
lily	die Lilie

lily of the valley	das Maiglöckchen
mignonette	die Reseda

134

snowdrop	das Schneeglöckchen
crocus	der Krokus
carnation	die Nelke
bluebell	die Glockenblume
poppy	der Mohn
cornflower	die Kornblume
buttercup	die Butterblume
daffodil	die Osterglocke
forget-me-not -	das Vergißmeinnicht

135

foxglove	der Fingerhut
sunflower	die Sonnenblume
dandelion	der Löwenzahn
snapdragon	das Löwenmaul
marigold	die Ringelblume
orchid	die Orchidee
bush	der Busch
magnolia	die Magnolie
fuchsia	die Fuchsie
rhododendron	der Rhododendrom

136

shrub	der Strauch
heather	das Heidekraut
undergrowth	das Unterholz
scrub	das Buschwerk
broom	der Ginster
mallow	die Malve
laurel	der Lorbeer
privet hedge	die Ligusterhecke
to enclose	einfassen

137

vegetables	das Gemüse *sing*
kitchen garden	der Küchengarten
mushroom	der Champignon
fungus	der Pilz
harmful	schädlich, giftig
leek	der Lauch
radish	das Radieschen
lettuce	der Salat
celery	der Staudensellerie
rhubarb	der Rhabarber

138

chard	der innere Blattstiel der Artischoke
spinach	der Spinat
turnip	die weiße Rübe
potato	die Kartoffel
to peel	schälen
to scrape	abkratzen
husk	die Hülse
to husk	enthülsen
cabbage	der Kohl
hedge	die Hecke

139

fruit	das Obst
fruit tree	der Obstbaum
to graft	aufpfropfen
graft	der Pfropfreis
to shake	schütteln
to prune	ausschneiden
pear tree	der Birnenbaum
pear	die Birne
apple tree	der Apfelbaum
cherry tree	der Kirschbaum

140

cherry	die Kirsche
plum	die Pflaume
plum tree	der Pflaumenbaum
prune	die Trockenpflaume
stone	der Stein
to stone	entsteinen
almond	die Mandel
almond tree	der Mandelbaum
peach	der Pfirsich
peach tree	der Pfirsichbaum

141

apricot	die Aprikose
apricot tree	der Aprikosenbaum
walnut	die Walnuß
walnut tree	der Walnußbaum
chestnut	die (Eß-)Kastanie
chestnut tree	der (Eß-)Kastanienbaum
hazelnut	die Haselnuß
hazelnut tree	der Haselstrauch
lemon	die Zitrone
lemon tree	der Zitronenbaum

142

orange tree	der Orangenbaum
olive	die Olive
olive tree	der Olivenbaum
date	die Dattel
date palm	die Dattelpalme
palm tree	die Palme
pomegranate	der Granatapfel
pomegranate tree	der Granatapfelbaum
banana tree	die Bananenstaude
pineapple	die Ananas

143

coconut	die Kokosnuß
coconut tree	die Kokospalme
sugar cane	das Zuckerrohr
yam	die Yamwurzel
lychee	die Litschi
kiwi	die Kiwi
ripe	reif
to ripen	reifen
juicy	saftig
strawberry	die Erdbeere

144

strawberry plant	die Erdbeerpflanze
medlar	die Mispel
medlar tree	der Mispelbaum
raspberry	die Himbeere
raspberry bush	der Himbeerbusch
blackcurrant	die schwarze Johannisbeere
currant bush	der Johannisbeerbusch
gooseberry	die Stachelbeere
grape	die Traube
raisin	die Rosine

145

vine	der Weinstock
vineyard	der Weingarten
vintner	der Winzer
grape harvest	die Traubenernte
to gather grapes	Trauben ernten
press	die Presse
to press	pressen
forest trees	die Waldbäume
wood	der Wald
jungle	der Dschungel

146

woody	waldig
wild, uncultivated	wild
ivy	der Efeu
to climb	klettern
creeping	kletternd, Klettter-
wisteria	die Glyzine
mistletoe	die Mistel
rosewood	das Rosenholz
juniper	der Wacholder
fern	der Farn

147

tree	der Baum
bark	die Rinde
branch	der Ast
twig	der Zweig
knot	der Knoten
tree ring	der Jahresring
trunk	der Stamm
oak	die Eiche
acorn	der Ahorn
holm oak	die Steineiche

148

beech	die Buche
ash	die Esche
elm	die Ulme
poplar	die Pappel
aspen	die Espe
lime	die Linde
birch	die Birke
fir	die Tanne
conifer	der Nadelbaum
coniferous	zapfentragend

149

cone	der Zapfen
pine	die Kiefer
hop	der Hopfen
monkey puzzle	die Schuppentanne
sycamore	der Bergahorn
maple	der Ahorn
holly	die Stechpalme
alder	die Erle
bamboo	der Bambus
eucalyptus	der Eukalyptus

150

acacia	die Akazie
rubber tree	der Gummibaum
mahogany	das Mahagoni
ebony	das Ebenholz
cedar	die Zeder
cactus	der Kaktus
cacao tree	der Kakaobaum
giant sequoia	der Mammutbaum
bonsai	der Bonsai
yew	die Eibe

151

weeping willow	die Trauerweide
azalea	die Azalee
catkin	das (Weiden-)Kätzchen
spore	die Spore
pollination	die Bestäubung
to pollinate	bestäuben
pollen	der Blütenstaub
to fertilise	befruchten
stock (species)	der Bestand
hybrid	die Hybride

152

environmental	ökologisch
environmentalist	Ökologe
environmentalism	Ökologie
pollution	die Umweltverschmutzung
conserve	schützen
conservation	der Umweltschutz
waste	die Verschwendung
to waste	verschwenden
rubbish	Abfall
rubbish tip	der Müllhaufen

153

sewage	das Abwasser
spill	das Überlaufen
poisonous	giftig
to poison	vergiften
industrial waste	der Industriemüll
toxic	toxisch
pollutant	das Umweltgift
to pollute	(die Umwelt) belasten
consumerism	die Konsumgesellschaft
consumerist	das Mitglied der Konsumge- sellschaft

154

to consume	verbrauchen
solar panel	Solarpanel
windmill	die Windmühle
wind energy	die Windenergie
wave energy	die Wellenenergie
wildlife	das Tierreich
harmful	schädlich

atmosphere	die Atmosphäre
smog	der Smog
unleaded petrol	das bleifreie Benzin

155

ecosystem	das Ökosystem
ecology	die Ökologie
ecologist	der Ökokloge
acid rain	der saure Regen
deforestation	die Entwaldung
to deforest	entwalden
rainforest	der Regenwald
underdeveloped	unterentwickelt
industrialised	industrialisiert
ozone layer	die Ozonschicht

156

oil slick	der Ölteppich
oil spill	die Öllache
greenhouse effect	der Treibhauseffekt
to recycle	recyceln
recycling	das Recycling
renewable	erneuerbar
fossil fuels	die fossilen Brennstoffe *pl*
resource	die Quelle, Ressource
landfill	die Deponie
to waste	verschwenden

157

decibel	das Dezibel
to soundproof	lärmdicht machen
radiation	die Strahlung
radioactive	radioaktiv
nuclear energy	die Kernenergie
fallout	der Fallout
reactor	der Reaktor

fission	die Spaltung
fusion	die Fusion
leak	das Leck

The Home   *Das Zuhause*

158

house	das Haus
apartment block	der Wohnblock
to let	vermieten
tenant	der Mieter
housing	der Wohnraum
to change	ändern
to move house	umziehen
landlord, owner	der Vermieter, der Eigentümer
own	eigen
ownership	das Eigentum

159

country house	das Landhaus
farmhouse	das Bauernhaus
villa	das Chalet
cottage	das Häuschen
chalet	das Chalet
terraced house	das Reihenhaus
semi-detached house	die Doppelhaushälfte
country house	das Landhaus
mansion	die Villa
palace	der Palast

160

castle	die Burg
igloo	der Iglu
teepee	das Tipi
log cabin	das Blockhaus
houseboat	das Hausboot

hut	die Hütte
house trailer	der Wohnwagen
penthouse	das Penthaus
lighthouse	der Leuchtturm
shack	der Verschlag

161
building	das Gebäude
to build	bauen
building site	das Baugelände
building contractor	der Bauunternehmer
repair	reparieren
solid	solide
to destroy	zerstören
to demolish	abreißen
garage	die Garage
shed	das Gartenhaus

162
door	die Tür
doorknocker	der Türdrücker
to knock at the door	an die Tür klopfen
doormat	der Fußabstreifer
doorbell	die Türklingel
threshold	die Schwelle
bolt	der Riegel
plan	der Plan
foundations	das Fundament
to found	gründen

163
cement	der Zement
concrete	der Beton
stone	der Stein
cornerstone	der Eckstein
angular	eckig

antiquated	veraltet
modern	modern
luxurious	luxuriös
roomy	geräumig
whitewashed	gekalkt
neglected	vernachlässigt

164

worm-eaten	vom Holzwurm befallen
moth-eaten	mottenzerfressen
shanty	der Schuppen
shantytown	die Wellblechhüttensiedlung
brick	der Backstein
sand	der Sand
slate	die Schindel
gutter	die Dachrinne
drainpipe	das Abflußrohr
step	die Stufe

165

plaster	der Verputz
skirting	die Fußleiste
floor	der Boden
wall	die Wand
partition wall	die Trennwand
wood	das Holz
board	das Brett
beam	der Balken
to sustain	stützen
to contain, hold	enthalten

166

facade	die Fassade
outside	die Außenseite
inside	die Innenseite
window	das Fenster

windowsill	das Fensterbrett
venetian blind	die Jalousie
shutter	der Fensterladen
balcony	der Balkon
windowpane	die Fensterscheibe
glass	das Glas

167

porch	der Eingang
door	die Tür
hinge	die Angel
front door	die Eingangstür
doorkeeper	der Pförtner
to open	öffnen
opening	die Öffnung
entrance	der Eingang
to enter	eintreten
to go out	ausgehen

168

way out	der Ausgang
lock	das Schloß
to shut, close	schließen
to lock up	zuschließen, verschließen
key	der Schlüssel
to lock	abschließen
staircase	das Treppenhaus
upstairs	oben
downstairs	unten
landing	die Diele

169

ladder	die Leiter
banisters	das Treppengeländer
lift	der Aufzug
to go up	nach oben gehen

to ascend	nach oben gehen
ascent	der Aufstieg
to go down	nach unten gehen
descent	der Abstieg
low	niedrig
storeys	die Stockwerke

170

ground floor	das Erdgeschoß
first floor	der erste Stock
cellar	der Keller
tile	die Kachel
roof	das Dach
ceiling	die Decke
floor	der Boden
to turn	(sich) drehen
to return	zurückkehren
return	die Rückkehr

171

to give back	zurückgeben
chimney	der Kamin
hearth	die Feuerstelle
fire	das Feuer
spark	der Funke
to sparkle	glitzern
flame	die Flamme
ashes	die Asche *sing*
stove	der Herd
smoke	der Rauch

172

to smoke (of fire)	rauchen
to burn	brennen
to blaze	lodern
ardent	lodernd

coal	die Kohle
charcoal	die Holzkohle
embers	die Glut
to scorch	versengen
to glow	glühen
firewood	das Feuerholz

173
woodcutter	der Holzhacker
shovel	die Schaufel
poker	dser Feuerhaken
to poke	stochern
matches	die Streichhölzer
wax	das Wachs
to light	anzünden
box	die Schachtel
drawer	die Schublade
chest of drawers	die Kommode

174
comfortable	bequem
uncomfortable	unbequem
lighting	die Beleuchtung
dazzle, splendour	das gleißende Licht
to light up	erleuchten
to put out, extinguish	löschen
light	das Licht
lamp	die Lampe
lampshade	der Lampenschirm
wick	der Docht

175
candle	die Kerze
candlestick	der Kerzenhalter
room	das Zimmer
to inhabit	bewohnen

inhabitant	der Bewohner
to reside	wohnen
residence	die Wohnung
hall (large room)	der Saal
furniture	die Möbel
a piece of furniture	ein Möbelstück

176

furnished	möbliert
corridor	der Flur
hall, lobby	die Eingangshalle
hall stand	der Garderobenständer
sitting room	das Wohnzimmer
lounge (of hotel)	das Foyer
to serve	einen Gast bedienen
guest	der Gast
to invite	einladen
table	der Tisch

177

seat	der Platz
to sit down	sich hinsetzen
to be sitting	sitzen
cushion	das Kissen
stool	der Hocker
chair	der Stuhl
armchair	der Sessel
rocking chair	der Schaukelstuhl
sofa	das Sofa
couch	die Couch
bench	die Bank

178

bookcase	der Bücherschrank
bookshelf	das Bücherregal
bookrest	die Buchstütze

library	die Bücherei
office, study	das Büro
writing desk	der Schreibtisch
to write	schreiben
handwriting	die Handschrift
paper	das Papier

179

record-player	der Plattenspieler
hi-fi	Hi-Fi
television	das Fernsehen
video recorder	der Videorekorder
radiator	der Heizkörper
radio	das Radio
ornament	das Ornament
clock	die Uhr
grandfather clock	die Standuhr

180

tapestry	die Gobelinstickerei
a tapestry	ein Wandbehand
to hang	aufhängen
to take down	abnehmen
wallpaper	die Tapete
to wallpaper	tapezieren
tile (decorative)	die (Zier-)Kachel
floor tile	die Bodenfließe
tiling	das Fließen
picture	das Bild

181

frame	der Rahmen
portrait	das Porträt
photograph	die Fotografie
photograph album	das Fotoalbum
dining room	das Eßzimmer

69

to eat, dine	essen
meals	die Mahlzeiten
breakfast	das Frühstück
to breakfast	frühstücken
lunch	das Mittagessen

182

dinner	das Abendessen
to lunch	zu Mittag essen
supper	das Abendessen
to have supper	zu Abend essen
sideboard	das Sideboard
larder	der Speiseschrank
pantry	die Speisekammer
shelf	das Regal
cup	die Tasse
draining board	das Abtropfbrett

183

sugarbowl	die Zuckerdose
coffeepot	die Kaffeekanne
teapot	die Teekanne
tray	das Tablett
table service	das Service
tablecloth	das Tischtuch
napkin	die Serviette
plate	der Teller
saucer	die Untertasse
serving dish	der Vorlegeteller

184

microwave	die Mikrowelle
to microwave	in der Mikrowelle kochen
food mixer	der Mixer
refrigerator	der Kühlschrank
grater	die Reibe

flowerpot	der Blumentopf
(drinking) glass	das Glas
glassware	das Glas
to cook	kochen
to boil	kochen

185

gas cooker	der Gasherd
electric cooker	der Elektroherd
grill	der Grill
barbecue grill	der Holkohlengrill
saucepan	die Kasserole
refuse, rubbish	der Abfall
washing machine	die Waschmaschine
sewing machine	die Nähmaschine
washing powder	das Waschpulver
vacuum cleaner	der Staubsauger

186

electricity	die Elektrizität
fusebox	der Sicherungskasten
central heating	die Zentralheizung
light bulb	die Glübirne
switch	der Schalter
to switch on	anschalten
to switch off	ausschalten
plug	der Stecker
socket	die Steckdose
air conditioning	die Klimaanlage

187

lid, cover	der Deckel
to cover	zudecken
to uncover	öffnen
to uncork	entkorken
crockery	das Geschirr

to cover	abdecken
discover	entdecken
spoon	der Löffel
teaspoon	der Teelöffel
spoonful	einen Löffel voll

188
fork	die Gabel
cutlery	das Besteck
set of cutlery	das Gedeck
knife	das Messer
to carve (meat)	tranchieren
to cut	schneiden
sharp	scharf
bottle	die Flasche
cork	der Korken
corkscrew	der Korkenzieher

189
to pull out	herausziehen
to drink	trinken
beverage, drink	das Getränk
to toast (health)	zuprosten
oven	die Röhre
(kitchen) utensils	die Küchengeräte *pl*
saucepan	die Kasserolle
frying pan	die Pfanne
pot	der Topf
pitcher	der Krug

190
bucket	der Eimer
to pour out	ausgießen
basket	der Korb
to fill	füllen
full	voll

empty	leer
to empty	leeren
broom	der Besen
to sweep	kehren
to rub	reiben
to scrub	schrubben

191

to wash (dishes)	abwaschen
bedroom (master bedroom)	das Schlafzimmer
(other) bedroom	das Zimmer
to go to bed	zu Bett gehen
bed	das Bett
bedspread	die Tagesdecke
bunk bed	das Stockbett
cot	das Kinderbett
mattress	die Matratze
sheets	die Bettücher *pl*
electric blanket	die elektrische Wärmdecke

192

bolster	die Schlummerrolle
pillow	das Kissen
carpet	der Teppich
rug, mat	der Vorleger
to wake	wecken
to awake	aufwachen
to get up early	früh aufstehen
the early hours	die Nacht, nach Mitternacht
curtain	der Vorhang
attic	die Mansarde

193

alarm clock	der Wecker
hot-water bottle	die Wärmflasche
nightcap	der Bettrunk

to sleepwalk	schlafwandeln
sleepwalker	der Schlafwandler, die Schlaf-wandlerin
sleepwalking	das Schlafwandeln
wardrobe	der Kleiderschrank
to keep, preserve	behalten
dressing table	der Schminktisch
screen	der Paravent

194

bathroom	das Badezimmer
bath	das Bad
bathtub	die Badewanne
to bathe	baden
to wash	waschen
to wash oneself	sich waschen
towel	das Handtuch
washbasin	das Waschbecken
shower	die Dusche
to take a shower	sich duschen

195

tap	der Wasserhahn
to turn on (tap)	(den Hahn) aufdrehen
to turn off (tap)	(den Hahn) abdrehen
sponge	der Schwamm
facecloth	der Waschlappen
toothbrush	die Zahnbürste
toothpaste	die Zahnpasta
toothpick	der Zahnstocher
toilet paper	das Eau de Toilette
toilet bowl	die Waschschüssel

196

soap	die Seife
shampoo	das Schampu

makeup	das Makeup
face cream	die Gesichtscreme
face pack	die Gesichtsmaske
compact	der Kompaktpulver
lipstick	der Lippenstift
nail file	die Nagelfeile
nail clippers	die Nagelschere
nail varnish	der Nagellack

197

hairpin	die Haarnadel
hairdryer	der Föhn
hairspray	das Haarspray
hairslide	die Haarklammer
hairpiece	das Haarteil
hairnet	das Haarnetz
to wipe	wischen
to clean	reinigen
clean	sauber
dirty	schmutzig

198

mirror	der Spiegel
basin	das Becken, die Schüssel
jug	der Krug
razor (cutthroat)	das Rasiermesser
smoke detector	der Feuermelder
razorblade	die Rasierklinge
electric razor	der Rasierapparat
shaving foam	der Rasierschaum
comb	der Kamm
to comb (oneself)	(sich) kämmen

199

tools	das Werkzeug
saw	die Säge

to saw	sägen
drill	die Bohrmaschine
drill bit	der Bohrer
sawdust	das Sägemehl
hammer	der Hammer
nail	der Nagel
to nail	nageln
spade	die Schaufel
pickaxe	die Spitzhacke

200

screw	die Schraube
screwdriver	der Schraubenzieher
axe	die Axt
paint	die Farbe
paintbrush	der Pinsel
to paint	malen, streichen
glue	der Leim
to glue, stick	leimen, kleben
sander	die Schleifmaschine
sandpaper	das Schleifpapier

Society   *Die Gesellschaft*

201

street	die Straße
walk, promenade	der Spaziergang
to go for a walk	spazierengehen
passer-by	der Passant, die Passantin
avenue	die Allee
kiosk	der Kiosk
native of	der Einwohner aus, die Einwohnerin aus
compatriot	der Landsmann, die Landsmännin

pavement	der Bürgersteig
gutter	die Gosse

202

road	die Straße
high road	die Hauptstraße
street lamp	die Straßenlampe
traffic	der Verkehr
frequented	besucht
to frequent	besuchen
pedestrian	der Fußgänger
pedestrian area	die Fußgängerzone
square	der Platz
park	der Park

203

crossroads	die Kreuzung
corner	die Ecke
alley	der Fußweg
quarter (of town)	das Viertel
slum	der Slum
outskirts	die Außenbezirke
around	um… herum
dormitory town	die Schlafstadt
premises	das Gelände
warehouse	das Lagerhaus

204

cul-de-sac	die Sackgasse
one-way	die Einbahnstraße
traffic jam	der Verkehrsstau
rush hour	die Stoßzeit
zebra crossing	der Zebrastreifen
shop window	das Schaufenster
poster	das Plakat
bus stop	die Bushaltestelle

to queue	sich anstellen
routine	die Routine

205

shop	der Laden
shopkeeper	der Ladenführer, die Ladenführerin
counter	die Theke
to show	zeigen
inn	die Gaststätte
innkeeper	der Gaststätteninhaber, die Gaststätteninhaberin
to stay	bleiben, wohnen
lodging house	die Pension
guest	der Gast
board and lodgings	Unterkunft und Verpflegung

206

profession	der Beruf
trade	das Gewerbe
mechanic	der Mechaniker, die Mechanikerin
engineer	der Techniker, die Technikerin
spinner	der Spinner, die Spinnerin
workman	der Arbeiter, die Arbeiterin
operative	der Bediener, die Bedienerin
apprentice	der Lehrling
apprenticeship	die Ausbildung, die Lehre
day labourer	der Tagelöhner

207

fireman	der Feuerwehrmann
fire station	die Feuerwehrstation
fire hydrant	der Hydrant
shop assistant	der Verkäufer, die Verkäuferin
fishmonger	der Fischverkäufer, die Fischverkäuferin
fishmonger's	der Fischladen

street sweeper	der Straßenkehrer, die Straßenkehrerin
library	die Bibliothek
librarian	der Bibliothekar, die Bibliothekarin
notary	der Notar, die Notarin

208

policeman	der Polizist, die Polizistin
police (force)	die Polizei
police station	die Polizeistation
secretary	der Sekretär, die Sekretärin
plumber	der Klempner, die Klempnerin
jeweller	der Juwelier, die Juwelierin
stonecutter	der Steinmetz, die Steinmetzin
hatter	der Hutmacher, die Hutmacherin
hat shop	der Hutladen

209

carpenter	der Zimmermann
ironmonger	der Eisenwarenhändler, die Eisenwarenhändlerin
miller	der Müller, die Müllerin
mill	die Mühle
to grind	mahlen
baker	der Bäcker, die Bäckerin
to knead	kneten
bakery	die Bäckerei
barber	der Friseur, die Friseurin
barbershop	der Frisiersalon

210

tobacconist	der Tabakwarenhändler, die Tabakwarenhändlerin
tobacconist's	das Tabakwarengeschäft, die Traffik (*Austria*)

rag-and-bone-man	der Lumpenhändler, die Lumpenhändlerin
tailor	der Schneider, die Schneiderin
tailor's	die Schneiderei
butcher	der Metzger, der Fleischer
butcher's	die Metzgerei, die Fleischerei
milkman	der Milchmann
dairy	die Molkerei
glazier	der Glasierer, die Glasiererin

211

bricklayer	der Maurer
stationer	der Papierwarenhändler, die Papierwarenhändlerin
stationer's	die Papierwarenhandlung
upholsterer	der Dekorateur
photographer	der Fotograf, die Fotografin
blacksmith	der Schmied
horseshoe	das Hufeisen
to shoe (horses)	behufen
shepherd	der Schafhirte, die Schafhirtin
cowboy	der Kuhhirte, die Kuhhirtin

212

farm	der Bauernhof
to lease	verpachten
country estate	das Landgut
courtyard	der Hof
well	der Brunnen
stable	der Stall
hayfork	die Heugabel
straw	das Stroh
hay	das Heu
haystack	der Heuhaufen
grain	das Korn

213

agriculture	die Landwirtschaft
agricultural	landwirtschaftlich
rustic	ländlich
countryside	die Landschaft, das Land
peasant	der Bauer, die Bäuerin
farmer	der Landwirt, die Landwirtin
to cultivate	anbauen
cultivation	der Anbau
tillage	das Pflügen
to plough	pflügen

214

plough	der Pflug
furrow	die Furche
fertiliser	der Dünger
to fertilise (crop)	düngen
fertile	fruchtbar
barren	unfruchtbar
dry	trocken
to sow	sähen
seed	der Samen
sowing	die Saat

215

to scatter	verstreuen
to germinate	keimen
to mow	mähen
reaper	der Erntearbeiter
reaping machine	die Erntemaschine
combine harvester	der Mähdrescher
sickle	die Sichel
scythe	die Sense
to harvest	ernten
harvest	die Ernte

216

rake	der Rechen
to rake	rechen
spade	die Schaufel
to dig	graben
hoe	die Hacke
meadow	die Wiese
silage	das Silofutter
wheat	der Weizen
oats	der Hafer
barley	die Gerste
ear (of wheat)	die (Weizen-)Ähre

217

maize	der Mais
rice	der Reis
alfalfa	das Alfalfa
pile	der Haufen
to pile up	aufhäufen
tractor	der Traktor
harrow	die Egge
baler	der Stabilistor
rotovator	der Pflug mit rotierenden Klingen
milking machine	die Melkmaschine

218

to milk	melken
stockbreeder	der Viehzüchter, die Viehzüchterin
stockbreeding	die Viehzucht
fodder, feed	das Futter
to irrigate	bewässern
greenhouse	das Treibhaus
subsidy	die Unterstützung
grape harvest	die Weinernte
grape picker	der Traubenpflücker

219

commerce	der Handel
firm	die Firma
branch	die Filiale
export	die Ausfuhr
import	die Einfuhr
company	die Gesellschaft
partner	der Partner
to associate	in Partnerschaft gehen
businessman	der Geschäftsmann
business	das Geschäft

220

subject	das Thema
to offer	bieten
offer	das Gebot
demand	die Forderung
account	das Konto
current account	das Girokonto
to settle	begleichen
order	der Auftrag
to cancel	annullieren
on credit	auf Kredit

221

by instalments	auf Raten
for cash	gegen Bargeld
market	der Markt
deposit	die Kaution
goods	die Waren
bargain	das Sonderangebot
second-hand	aus zweiter Hand
cheap	billig
expensive	teuer
to bargain, haggle	handeln

222

packaging	die Verpackung
to pack up	einpacken
to unpack	auspacken
to wrap	einwickeln
to unwrap	auswickeln
transport	der Transport
to transport	transportieren
carriage	der Wagen
portable	tragbar
delivery	die Lieferung

223

to deliver	liefern
to dispatch	absenden
office	das Büro
manager	der Manager, die Managerin
accountant	der Buchhalter, die Buchhalterin
clerk	der Angestellte, die Angestellte
to depend on	abhängig sein von
to employ	einstellen
employee	der Arbeitnehmer, die Arbeitnehmerin
employment	die Anstellung

224

employer	der Arbeitgeber, die Arbeitgeberin
unemployment	die Arbeitslosigkeit
unemployed	arbeitslos
chief	der Chef, die Chefin
typewriter	die Schreibmaschine
typist	die Schreibkraft
typing	das Maschinenschreiben
shorthand	die Stenographie
shorthand typist	der Stenotypist, die Stenotypistin
audiotypist	der Audiotypist, die Audiotypistin

225

director	das Vorstandsmitglied
managing director	der geschäftsführende Direktor, die geschäftsführende Direktorin
board of directors	der Vorstand
shareholder	der Aktionär, die Aktionärin
dividend	die Dividende
takeover	die Übernahme
to list (shares)	Aktien notieren lassen
asset	das Vermögen
liability	die Verbindlichkeiten *pl*
contract	der Vertrag

226

purchase	der Kauf
to buy	kaufen
sell	verkaufen
sale	der Verkauf
buyer	der Käufer, die Käuferin
seller	der Verkäufer, die Verkäuferin
wholesale	(der Verkauf) en gros
to bid	bieten
bidder	der Steigerer

227

to auction	versteigern
client	der Kunde, die Kundin
clientele	die Kundschaft
catalogue	der Katalog
price	der Preis
quantity	die Menge
gross	bruto
net	netto
to cost	kosten
cost	die Kosten *pl*

228

free of charge	kostenlos
pay	zahlen
wages	der Lohn
salary	das Gehalt
payment	die Bezahlung
in advance	im voraus
invoice	die Rechnung
checkout	die Kasse
cashier	der Kassierer, die Kassiererin
accounts	die Konten

229

balance sheet	die Bilanz
general income	die Einnahmen
expenditure	die Ausgaben
to spend	ausgeben
to acknowledge receipt	quittieren
to receive	erhalten
reception	der Empfang
profit	der Gewinn
loss	der Verlust
loan	das Darlehn

230

to borrow	borgen
to lend	leihen
to prepare	vorbereiten
to obtain	erhalten
creditor	der Gläubiger
debt	die Schuld
debtor	der Schuldner
to get into debt	Schulden machen
to be in debt	verschuldet sein
bankruptcy	der Konkurs

231

to go bankrupt	in Konkurs gehen
banking	das Bankwesen
bank	die Bank
banknote	der Geldschein
banker	der Bankier
bankbook	das Bankbuch
bankcard	die Kreditkarte
bank account	das Bankkonto
savings bank	die Sparkasse

232

to save (money)	sparen
capital	das Kapital
interest	das Vermögen
income	das Einkommen
stock exchange	die Börse
share	die Aktie
shareholder	der Aktionär
exchange	der Kurs
rate	der Satz
to exchange	wechseln
exchange rate	der Wechselkurs

233

to be worth	wert sein
value	der Wert
to value	bewerten
discount	der Rabatt
to deduct	abziehen
to cash a cheque	einen Scheck einlösen
payable on sight	auf Sicht zahlbar
signature	die Unterschrift
to sign	unterschreiben
draft	der Wechsel

234

postal order	die Postanweisung
to fall due	fällig werden
date	das Datum
to date	datieren
to inform	unterrichten
warning	die Warnung
coin	die Münze
money	das Geld
mint	die Münzstätte

235

post office	das Postamt
mail	die Post
by return of post	postwendend
postcard	die Postkarte
letter	der Brief
postman	der Briefträger
letterbox	der Briefkasten
collection	die Abholung
to collect	abholen
delivery	die Lieferung

236

to distribute	verteilen
distributor	der Verteiler
envelope	der Umschlag
postage	das Beförderungsentgelt
to frank	frankieren
to seal	versiegeln
stamp	der Stempel
postmark	der Poststempel
to stamp	mit Briefmarken versehen
to pack	verpacken
to unpack	auspacken

237

to register	einschreiben
to forward	zustellen
sender	der Sender
addressee	der Adressat
unknown	unbekannt
to send	senden
price list	der Tarif
courier	der Bote
air mail	die Luftpost
by airmail	per Luftpost

238

pound sterling	Pfund Sterling
franc	der Franc (*France*), der Franken (*Switzerland*)
mark	die Mark
dollar	der Dollar
penny	der Penny
shilling	der Schilling
ingot	der (Gold-)Barren
foreign currencies	die Fremdwährung
speculation	die Spekulation
speculator	der Spekulant

239

wealthy	wohlhabend
wealth	der Reichtum
rich	reich
to get rich	reich werden
to acquire	erwerben
to possess	besitzen
fortune	das Vermögen
to be fortunate	Glück haben
poverty	die Armut

poor	arm
necessity	die Notwendigkeit

240

to need	brauchen
misery	das Elend
miserable	elend
beggar	der Bettler, die Bettlerin
to beg	betteln
homeless	obdachlos
squatter	der Hausbesetzer, die Hausbesetzerin
eviction	die Räumung
malnourished	unterernährt
disadvantaged	unterprivilegiert

241

industry	die Industrie, die Branche
industrialist	der Industrielle
manufacture	die Produktion
to manufacture	produzieren, herstellen
factory	die Fabrik
manufacturer	der Produzent
trademark	das Warenzeichen
machine	die Maschine
machinery	die Maschinerie
to undertake	unternehmen

242

enterprise	das Unternehmen
expert	der Experte
skill	die Fertigkeit
skilful	fähig
ability	die Fähigkeit
clumsy	ungeschickt
to keep busy	sich beschäftigen
busy	beschäftigt

lazy	faul
strike	der Streik

243

striker	der Streikteilnehmer, die Streikteilnehmerin
lock-out	die Aussperrung
blackleg	der Streikbrecher, die Streikbrecherin
picket	der Streikposten
to go on strike	in Streik gehen
trade union	die Gewerkschaft
trade unionist	der Gewerkschaftler, die Gewerkschaftlerin
trade unionism	die Gewerkschaftsbewegung
minimum wage	der Mindestlohn
market economy	die Marktwirtschaft

244

government	die Regierung
to govern	regieren
politics	die Politik
political	politisch
politician	der Politiker, die Politikerin
socialist	sozialistisch
conservative	konservativ
liberal	liberal
fascist	faschistisch
communist	kommunistisch

245

monarchy	die Monarchie
monarch	der Monarch
king	der König
queen	die Königin
viceroy	der Vizekönig

to reign	regieren
royal	königlich
crown	die Krone
to crown	krönen
throne	der Thron

246
court	der Hof
courtier	der Höfling
chancellor	der Kanzler
rank	der Rang
prince	der Prinz
princess	die Prinzessin
title	der Titel
subject	der Untertan, die Untertanin
emperor	der Kaiser
empress	die Kaiserin

247
revolution	die Revolution
guillotine	die Guillotine
to guillotine	guillotinieren
counterrevolution	die Konterrevolution
aristocracy	die Aristokratie
aristocrat	der Aristokrat
confiscate	konfiszieren
confiscation	die Konfiszierung
secular	weltlich
secularisation	die Verweltlichung

248
republic	die Republik
republican	republikanisch
president	der Präsident
embassy	die Botschaft
ambassador	der Botschafter, die Botschafterin

consul	der Konsul, die Konsulin
consulate	das Konsulat
state	der Staat
city state	der Stadtstaat
councillor	das Ratsmitglied

249

council	der Rat
to advise	beraten
to administer	verwalten
minister	der Minister, die Ministerin
ministry	das Ministerium
cabinet	das Kabinett
deputy	der Gesandte, die Gesandte
parliament	das Parlament
senate	der Senat
senator	der Senator, die Senatorin

250

session	die Sitzung
to deliberate	sich beraten
dialogue	der Dialog
discuss	diskutieren
adopt	adoptieren
decree	der Beschluß
to decree	beschließen
to proclaim	ausrufen
election	die Wahl
referendum	die Volksabstimmung

251

to elect	wählen
vote	wählen
vote	die Stimme
town council	der Gemeinderat
mayor	der Bürgermeister

bailiff	der Gerichtsvollzieher, die Gerichtsvollzieherin
justice	die Gerechtigkeit
just	gerecht
unjust	ungerecht
judge	der Richter, die Richterin

252
to judge	richten
court	das Gericht
judgment	das Urteil
injury	die Verletzung
to protect	schützen
law	das Gesetz
legal	legal
illegal	illegal
to bequeath	vererben
beneficiary	der Begünstigte, die Begünstigte

253
to make a will	sein Testament machen
will	das Testament
heir	der Erbe
heiress	die Erbin
to inherit	erben
inheritance	die Erbschaft
tribunal	die Gerichtsverhandlung
to summons	vorladen
summons	die Vorladung
appointment	die Bestellung

254
trial	der Prozeß
lawsuit	das Gerichtsverfahren
lawyer	der Rechtsanwalt
to advocate	verteidigen

to swear	schwören
oath	der Eid
witness	der Zeuge, die Zeugin
to bear witness	bezeugen
testimony	das Zeugnis
evidence	der Beweis

255

to infringe	übertreten
indictment	die Anklage
to plead	plädieren
to accuse	anklagen
accused	der Beklagte, die Beklagte
plaintiff	der Kläger, die Klägerin
defendant	der Angeklagte, die Angeklagte
to sue	verklagen
fault	die Schuld
jury	die Geschworenen *pl*

256

crime	das Verbrechen
murderer	der Mörder, die Mörderin
to murder	ermorden
murder	der Mord
to kill	töten
suicide	der Selbstmord
to commit	begehen
offence	eine Straftat
thief	der Dieb, die Diebin
bandit	der Bandit, die Banditin

257

theft	der Diebstahl
to steal	stehlen
traitor	der Verräter, die Verräterin
treason	der Verrat

fraud	der Betrug
bigamy	die Bigamie
bigamist	der Bigamist, die Bigamistin
assault	die Körperverletzung
blackmail	die Erpressung
to blackmail	erpressen

258
rape	die Vergewaltigung
rapist	der Vergewaltiger
guilty	schuldig
innocent	unschuldig
defence	die Verteidigung
to defend	verteidigen
to prohibit	verbieten
acquittal	der Freispruch
to acquit	freisprechen

259
sentence	das Urteil
to sentence	verurteilen
verdict	der Urteilspruch
fine	die Geldbuße
conviction	die Schuldigsprechung
to condemn	schuldig sprechen
prison	das Gefängnis, die Justiz-vollzugsanstalt
to imprison	einsperren
prisoner	der Gefangene, die Gefangene
to arrest	verhaften

260
capital punishment	die Todesstrafe
executioner	der Henker, die Henkerin
gallows	der Galgen
firing squad	das Schießkommando

electric chair	der elektrische Stuhl
pardon	die Begnadigung
remission	der Erlaß
parole	die bedingte Strafaussetzung
false imprisonment	die Freiheitsberaubung
self-defence	die Selbstverteidigung

261

army	die Armee
to drill	exerzieren
military	militärisch
soldier	der Soldat, die Soldatin
conscription	die Einberufung
conscript	der Wehrdienstpflichtige
conscientious objector	der Wehrdienstverweigerer
recruit	der Rekrut, die Rekrutin
flag	die Fahne
troops	die Truppe

262

officer	der Offizier, die Offizierin
sergeant	der Feldwebel
corporal	der Korporal
rank	der Rang
general	der General
colonel	der Oberst
captain	der Kapitän
lieutenant	der Leutnant
discipline	die Disziplin
order	die Ordnung

263

disorder	die Unordnung
infantry	die Infanterie
cavalry	die Kavallerie
artillery	die Artillerie

cannon	die Kanone
grenade	die Granate
to explode	explodieren
gunpowder	das Schwarzpulver
ammunition	die Munition
bomb	die Bombe

264
to shell	bombardieren
bombardment	die Bombardierung
guard, watch	die Wache
sentry	der Wachposten
garrison	die Garnison
barracks	die Kaserne *sing*
regiment	das Regiment
detachment	die Abkommandierung
reinforcement	die Verstärkung
battalion	das Battallion

265
to equip	ausrüsten
equipment	die Ausrüstung
uniform	die Uniform
flak jacket	die schußsichere Weste
firearm	die Schußwaffe
to arm	bewaffnen
to disarm	entwaffnen
to load	beladen
to unload	entladen
to shoot	schießen

266
shot	der Schuß
bullet	die Kugel
bulletproof	kugelsicher
cartridge	die Kartusche

revolver	der Revolver
bayonet	das Bayonet
dagger	der Dolch
tank	der Panzer
armoured car	der Panzerwagen
barbed wire	der Stacheldraht

267
cold war	der kalte Krieg
superpower	die Supermacht
rocket	die Rakete
nuclear warhead	der Atomsprengkopf
blockade	die Blockade
holocaust	der Holocaust
friendly fire	das Freundesfeuer
ceasefire	der Waffenstillstand
disarmament	die Abrüstung
pacifism	der Pazifismus

268
war	der Krieg
warlike	kriegerisch
warrior	der Krieger
guerrilla	die Guerilla, der Guerillero
guerrilla campaign	der Guerillakampf
siege	die Belagerung
to besiege	belagern
fort	das Fort
spy	der Spion, die Spionin

269
attack	der Angriff
to attack	angreifen
assault	der Überfall
ambush	der Ambusch
to surrender	sich ergeben

surrender	die Ergebung
encounter	das Treffen
to meet	treffen
fight	der Kampf
to fight	kämpfen

270

combatant	der Kämpfer
exploit	das Ergebnis
battlefield	das Schlachtfeld
trench	der Graben
to repel	abschrecken
retreat	sich zurückziehen
flight	die Flucht
to flee	fliehen
defeat	die Niederlage
to defeat	besiegen

271

to pursue	verfolgen
pursuit	die Verfolgung
to conquer	erobern
victor	der Sieger, die Siegerin
vanquished	der Unterlegene
armistice	der Waffenstillstand
treaty	das Abkommen
peace	der Frieden
captivity	die Gefangenschaft
to escape	entkommen

272

to encamp	lagern
encampment	das Lager
to manoeuvre	manövrieren
manoeuvre	das Manöver
wounded	verwundet

hero	der Held
heroine	die Heldin
medal	die Medaille
pension	die Rente
war memorial	das Kriegerdenkmal

273

navy	die Marine
sailor	der Matrose
admiral	der Admiral
squadron	das Schwadron
fleet	die Flotte
to float	treiben
to sail	segeln
navigator	der Steuermann
warship	das Kriegsschiff
battleship	das Kampfschiff

274

aircraft carrier	der Flugzeugträger
fighter plane	das Kampfflugzeug
destroyer	der Zerstörer
minesweeper	das Minenräumboot
submarine	das U-Boot
aerodrome	der Flughafen
spotter plane	das Aufklärungsflugzeug
air raid	der Luftangriff
to bomb	bombardieren
parachute	der Fallschirm

275

parachutist	der Fallschirmspringer, die Fallschirmspringerin
surface to air missile	das Land-Luft-Geschoß
helicopter	der Helikopter
to bring down	abschießen

anti-aircraft gun	das Flugabwehrgeschütz
shelter	der Bunker
bomb disposal	die Entschärfung von Bomben
bomber (plane)	der Bomber
to explode	explodieren
explosion	die Explosion

276

religion	die Religion
religious	religiös
God	Gott
god	der Gott
goddess	die Göttin
monk	der Mönch
nun	die Nonne
divine	göttlich
omnipotent	allmächtig
saviour	der Erlöser

277

safe	sicher
pagan	heidnisch
Christianity	das Christentum
Christian	der Christ, die Christin
Catholic	katholisch
Catholicism	der Katholizismus
Protestantism	der Protestantismus
Protestant	protestantisch
Calvinism	der Calvinismus
Calvinist	calvinistisch

278

Presbyterian	presbiterianisch
Mormonism	das Mormonentum
Mormon	der Mormone, die Mormonin
Bible	die Bibel

Koran	der Koren
Islam	der Islam
Muslim	mohamedanisch
Hindu	hinduistisch
Hinduism	der Hinduismus
Buddhist	buddhistisch

279

Buddhism	der Buddhismus
Jewish	jüdisch
Judaism	das Judentum
Rastafarian	rastafarian
scientology	(die) Scientology
to convert	konvertieren
sect	die Sekte
animism	der Animismus
voodoo	(das) Voodoo

280

shaman	der Schamane
atheist	der Atheist, die Atheistin
atheism	der Atheismus
agnostic	der Agnostiker
agnosticism	das Agnostikertum
heretic	der Ketzer, die Ketzerin
heresy	die Ketzerei
fundamentalist	der Fundamentalist, die Fundamentalistin
fundamentalism	der Fundamentalismus
to believe	glauben

281

believer	der/die Gläubige
belief	der Glaube
faith	der Glaube
church	die Kirche

chapel	die Kapelle
chalice	der Kelch
altar	der Altar
mass	die Messe
blessing	der Segen
to bless	segnen

282

to curse	verfluchen
clergy	der Klerus
clergyman	der Kleriker
to preach	predigen
preacher	der Prediger
sermon	die Predigt
apostle	der Apostel
angel	der Engel
holy	heilig
saint	der Heilige, die Heilige

283

blessed	selig
sacred	heilig
devil	der Teufel
devilish	teuflisch
cult	der Kult
solemn	feierlich
prayer	das Gebet
to pray	beten
devout	fromm
fervent	hingebungsvoll

284

sin	die Sünde
to sin	sündigen
sinner	der Sündiger, die Sündigerin
repentant	reumütig

to baptise	taufen
pope	der Papst
cardinal	der Kardinal
bishop	der Bischof
archbishop	der Erzbischof
priest	der Priester, die Priesterin

285
parish	die Gemeinde
abbot	der Abt
abbess	die Äbtissin
abbey	die Abtei
convent	das Kloster
monastery	das Kloster
minister	der Pfarrer, die Pfarrerin
pilgrim	der Pilgerer, die Pilgerin
pilgrimage	die Pilgerschaft
to celebrate	feiern

The Intellect and Emotions
Der Intellekt und die Emotionen

286
mind	der Geist
thought	der Gedanke
to think of	denken an
to meditate	meditieren
to remember	sich erinnern an
to agree with	übereinstimmen mit
agreement	die Übereinstimmung
soul	die Seele
to occur, come to mind	einfallen
recollection	die Erinnerung

287

renown	berühmt
to perceive	wahrnehmen
to understand	verstehen
understanding	das Verständnis
intelligence	die Intelligenz
intelligent	intelligent
clever	klug
stupid	dumm
stupidity	die Dummheit
worthy	würdig

288

unworthy	unwürdig
reason	die Vernunft
reasonable	vernünftig
unreasonable	unvernünftig
to reason	erwägen
to discuss	diskutieren
to convince	überzeugen
opinion	die Meinung
to affirm	bejahen
to deny	verneinen

289

certainty	die Gewißheit
certain	gewiß
uncertain	ungewiß
sure	sicher
unsure	unsicher
security	die Sicherheit
to risk	riskieren
doubt	der Zweifel
doubtful	zweifelhaft
mistake	der Fehler

290

to make a mistake	einen Fehler machen
suspicion	der Verdacht
to suspect	verdächtigen
suspicious	verdächtig
desire	die Sehnsucht
to desire	ersehnen
to grant	gewähren
will	der Wille
to decide	entscheiden
undecided	unentschlossen

291

to hesitate	zögern
capable	fähig
incapable	unfähig
capability	die Fähigkeit
talent	das Talent
disposition, temper	die Veranlagung, das Temperament
character	der Charakter
to rejoice	sich freuen
cheerfulness	die Fröhlichkeit
happiness	das Glück

292

cheerful	fröhlich
sad	traurig
sadness	die Traurigkeit
to grieve	trauern
enjoyment	der Genuß
happy	glücklich
unhappy	unglücklich
unfortunate	unglücklich
contented	zufrieden
discontented	unzufrieden

293

discontent	die Unzufriedenheit
displeased	unerfreut
pleasure	das Vergnügen
to please	gefallen
to displease	mißfallen
pain	der Schmerz
painful	schmerzhaft
sigh	der Seufzer
to sigh	seufzen
to complain	sich beschweren

294

complaint	die Beschwerde
to protest	protestieren
depressed	deprimiert
to despair	verzweifeln
despair	die Verzweiflung
hope	die Hoffnung
to hope	hoffen
expectation	die Erwartung
consolation	der Trost
to comfort	trösten

295

consoling	tröstlich
calm	die Ruhe
calm	ruhig
restless	rastlos
anxiety	die Angst, die Unruhe
fear	die Angst, die Furcht
to fear	fürchten
to be afraid	Angst haben
to frighten	erschrecken
to be frightened	Angst haben

296

terror	der Schrecken, der Terror
to terrify	erschrecken
frightful	ängstlich
to astonish	erstaunen
astonishment	das Erstaunen
to encourage	ermuntern
to discourage	abraten
conscience	das Gewissen
scruple	der Skrupel
remorse	die Reue

297

repentance	die Buße
to repent	büßen
to regret	bedauern
sentiment	das Gefühl
consent	die Zustimmung
to consent	zustimmen
mercy	die Gnade
charitable	nächstenliebend
pity	das Mitleid
piety	die Frömmigkeit

298

impiety	die Gottlosigkeit
friendly	freundlich
unfriendly	unfreundlich
favour	der Gefallen
to favour	begünstigen
favourable	günstig
unfavourable	ungünstig
confidence	das Vertrauen
trustful	vertrauensvoll
mistrustful	mißtrauisch

299

to trust	vertrauen
friendship	die Freundschaft
friendly	freundlich
kind	nett
friend	der Freund
enemy	der Feind
hatred	der Haß
to hate	hassen
hateful	verhaßt
contempt	die Verachtung

300

to despise	verachten
to get angry	ärgerlich werden
quarrel	der Streit
to quarrel	streiten
to reconcile	sich versöhnen
quality	die Qualität, die Eigenschaft
virtue	die Tugend
virtuous	tugendhaft
vice	das Laster
vicious	bösartig

301

addicted	abhängig
defect	der Mangel
fault	der Fehler
I lack, fail	mir fehlt
custom	die Sitte
to be necessary	nötig sein
to become accustomed	sich daran gewöhnen
habit	die Gewohnheit
to boast (about something)	sich (einer Sache) rühmen
moderate	gemäßigt

302

goodness	die Güte
good	gut
wickedness	die Schlechtigkeit
gratitude	die Dankbarkeit
ingratitude	die Undankbarkeit
grateful	dankbar
ungrateful	undankbar
to thank	danken
thanks, thank you	danke

303

honesty	die Ehrlichkeit
honourable	ehrbar
to honour	ehren
to dishonour	beleidigen
honour	die Ehre
dishonour	die Ehrlosigkeit
honest	ehrlich
dishonest	unehrlich

304

modesty	die Bescheidenheit
shame	die Scham
shameful	schamhaft
to be ashamed	sich schämen
audacity	die Kühnheit
audacious	kühn
daring	waghalsig
boldness	Wagemut
fearless	furchtlos
to dare	wagen

305

reckless	achtlos
timid	ängstlich

timidity	die Ängstlichkeit
rude	unverschämt
rudeness	die Unverschämtheit
courtesy	die Höflichkeit
polite	höflich
impolite	unhöflich
villain	der Bösewicht
envy	der Neid

306

loyal	loyal
disloyal	unloyal
generous	großzügig
generosity	die Großzügigkeit
selfishness	der Egoismus
selfish	egoistisch
egoist	der Egoist
greed	die Habsucht
stingy	geizig
miser	der Geizhals

307

truth	die Wahrheit
true	wahr
to lie	lügen
liar	der Lügner
lie	die Lüge
hypocritical	scheinheilig
hypocrite	der Scheinheilige
frank	offen
frankness	die Offenheit
accuracy	die Genauigkeit

308

inaccuracy	die Ungenauigkeit
punctuality	die Pünktlichkeit

faithfulness	die Treue
unfaithfulness	die Untreue
faithful	treu
unfaithful	untreu
coward	der Feigling
cowardice	die Feigheit
anger	der Ärger
offence	die Kränkung

309

to offend	kränken
to insult	beleidigen
excuse	die Entschuldigung
to excuse	entschuldigen
humble	demütig
humility	die Demut
pride	der Stolz
proud	stolz
vain	eingebildet
obstinate	starrköpfig

310

obstinacy	die Starrköpfigkeit
whim	die Laune
sober	nüchtern
sobriety	die Nüchternheit
sensual	sinnlich
sensuality	die Sinnlichkeit
hedonistic	hedonistisch
lust	die Lust
revenge	die Rache
to revenge	rächen

311

vindictive	rachsüchtig
jealous	eifersüchtig

temperamental	eigenwillig
affectionate	liebevoll
imaginative	phantasievoll
extrovert	extrovertiert
introvert	introvertiert
demanding	anspruchsvoll
sincere	ehrlich
sincerity	die Ehrlichkeit

312

optimistic	optimistisch
optimist	der Optimist
pessimistic	pessimistisch
pessimist	der Pessimist
perceptive	einfühlsam
cautious	wachsam
sensitive	sensibel
sensitivity	die Sensibilität
sensible	vernünftig
common sense	der gesunde Menschenverstand

Education and Learning
Die Erziehung und das Lernen

313

to educate	erziehen, bilden
educational	erzieherisch
educationalist	der Pädagoge, die Pädagogin
adult education	die Erwachsenenbildung
mixed education	die gemischte Erziehung
primary school	die Grundschule
to teach	lehren, unterrichten
teacher	der Lehrer, die Lehrerin
tutor	der Tutor, die Tutorin
college	das Kolleg

314

university	die Universität
class	die Klasse
pupil	der Schüler
boarder	der Internatsschüler
day pupil	der Tagesschüler
to study	studieren
student	der Student, die Studentin
grant	das Stipendium
scholarship holder	der Stipendiat
desk	der Schreibtisch

315

blackboard	die Tafel
chalk	die Kreide
pencil	der Bleistift
ink	die Tinte
pen	der Federhalter
ruler	das Lineal
line	die Zeile
exercise book	das Schreibheft
to bind (books)	(Bücher) einbinden
page	die Seite

316

to fold	falten
sheet of paper	das Blatt Papier
cover (book)	der Umschlag
work	die Arbeit
to work	arbeiten
hard-working	arbeitsam
studious	lernbegierig
lesson	die Lektion
to learn	lernen
to forget	vergessen

317

forgetful	vergeßlich
forgetfulness	die Vergeßlichkeit
absentminded	abwesend
course	der Kurs
attention	die Aufmerksamkeit
to be attentive	aufpassen
attentive	aufmerksam
inattentive	unaufmerksam
to explain	erklären
explanation	die Erklärung

318

task	die Aufgabe
theme	das Thema
thematic	thematisch
exercise	die Übung
to exercise	üben
practice	die Übung
to practise	üben
easy	leicht
easiness	die Leichtigkeit
difficult	schwierig

319

difficulty	die Schwierigkeit
progress	der Fortschritt
homework	die Hausaufgabe
must	müssen
to owe	schulden
examination	die Prüfung
to sit an examination	eine Prüfung machen
to pass an examination	eine Prüfung bestehen
to copy	kopieren
to swot	abschreiben

320

to examine	prüfen
examiner	der Prüfer
proof	der Beweis
to try	versuchen
to blame	beschuldigen
blame	die Beschuldigung
approve	billigen
disapprove	mißbilligen
mark	die Note
to note	anmerken

321

annotation	die Anmerkung
remarkable	bemerkenswert
prize	der Preis
to reward	belohnen
to praise	loben
praise	das Lob
holidays	die Ferien
vacancy	die freie Stelle
conduct	das Verhalten
to behave	sich verhalten

322

effort	die Bemühung
to endeavour	sich anstrengen
to try	versuchen
obedience	die Folgsamkeit
disobedience	die Unfolgsamkeit
obedient	folgsam
disobedient	unfolgsam
to obey	gehorchen
to disobey	nicht gehorchen
laziness	die Faulheit

323

strict	streng
severity	die Strenge
threat	die Drohung
to threaten	drohen
punishment	die Strafe
to punish	bestrafen
to deserve	verdienen
grammar	die Grammatik
to indicate	anzeigen
indication	der Hinweis

324

to point out something	auf etwas hinweisen
spelling	die Rechtschreibung
to spell	schreiben
full stop	der Punkt
colon	der Doppelpunkt
semicolon	der Strichpunkt
comma	das Komma
question mark	das Fragezeichen
exclamation mark	das Ausrufezeichen
to note down	notieren

325

to ask (question)	fragen
to ask for	bitten um
to answer	antworten
answer	die Antwort
to admire	bewundern
admiration	die Bewunderung
to exclaim	ausrufen
article	der Artikel
noun	das Hauptwort, das Substantiv
to name	nennen

326

appointment	die Verabredung
to call	rufen
to be called	heißen
reference	Hinweis
to relate to	sich beziehen auf
fixed	fest
to fix	festlegen
to join	sich zusammentun
together	gemeinsam
join	die Verbindung

327

to correspond	korrespondieren
correspondence	der Briefwechsel, die Korrespondenz
sentence	der Satz
language	die Sprache
idiomatic	idiomatisch
idiom	die Wendung
speech	die Sprache
talkative	gesprächig
voice	die Stimme
word	das Wort

328

to express	ausdrücken
expressive	ausdrucksvoll
vocabulary	das Vokabular
dictionary	das Wörterbuch
letter	der Brief
speech	die Rede
lecture	die Vorlesung
lecturer	der Lektor
orator	der Redner
eloquence	die Beredsamkeit

329

eloquent	beredsam
elocution	die Vortragskunst
to converse	sich unterhalten
conversation	die Unterhaltung
to understand	verstehen
to pronounce	aussprechen
to correct	korrigieren, verbessern
example	das Beispiel
meaning	die Bedeutung
to mean	bedeuten

330

translation	die Übersetzung
to translate	übersetzen
translator	der Übersetzer
interpreter	der Dolmetscher
to interpret	dolmetschen
interpretative	interpretierend
interpretation	die Interpretation
to imagine	sich vorstellen
imagination	die Vorstellungskraft

331

idea	die Idee
essay	der Aufsatz, der Essai
essayist	der Essayist
thesis	die These
doctorate	die Promovierung
to develop	entwickeln
to roll up	aufrollen
roll	die Rolle
object	der Gegenstand, das Objekt
subject	das Subjekt
describe	beschreiben

332

description	die Beschreibung
fable	die Fabel
drama	das Drama
comedy	die Komödie
comical	komisch
chapter	das Kapitel
to interest	interessieren
interesting	interessant
attractive	attraktiv
to attract	anziehen

333

to publish	veröffentlichen
to print	drucken
printer	der Drucker
printing	der Druck
newspaper	die Zeitung
journalist	der Journalist, die Journalistin
magazine	das Magazin
news	die Nachrichten
to announce	ankündigen
advertisement	die Werbung

334

history	die Geschichte
historian	der Historiker
the Stone Age	die Steinzeit
the Bronze Age	die Bronzezeit
the Iron Age	die Eisenzeit
the Dark Ages	das dunkle Mittelalter
the Middle Ages	das Mittelalter
archaeology	die Archäologie
archaeologist	der Archäologe
to excavate	ausgraben

335

carbon dating	die Radiokohlenstoffdatierung
event	das Ereignis
to happen	sich ereignen
to civilise	zivilisieren
civilisation	die Zivilisation
knight	der Ritter
chivalry	die Ritterlichkeit
explorer	der Entdecker
to explore	erforschen
discovery	die Entdeckung

336

to discover	entdecken
pirate	der Pirat
piracy	die Piraterie
treasure	der Schatz
conquest	die Eroberung
conqueror	der Eroberer
to conquer	erobern
empire	das Reich
imperial	kaiserlich, souverän
slave	der Sklave

337

emancipation	die Emanzipation
to emancipate	emanzipieren
destiny	das Schicksal
to destine	bestimmen
power	die Macht
powerful	mächtig
to be able, can	können, vermögen
slavery	die Sklaverei
to free	befreien
reformation	die Reformation

338

liberator	der Befreier
nationalism	der Nationalismus
nationalist	der Nationalist
alliance	die Allianz
to ally	sich allieren
ally	der Alliierte
to enlarge	vergrößern
increase	die Zunahme
to increase	zunehmen
to diminish	abnehmen

339

decline	der Untergang
to decay	verfallen
to decline	untergehen
to disturb	stören
to emigrate	auswandern
emigrant	der Auswanderer
rebel	der Rebell
rebellion	die Rebellion
rising	der Aufstand
independence	die Unabhängigkeit

340

geography	die Geographie
map	die Karte
North Pole	der Nordpol
South Pole	der Südpol
north	der Norden
south	der Süden
east	der Osten
west	der Westen
compass	der Kompaß
magnetic north	der magnetische Norden

341

distant	entfernt
distance	die Entfernung
near	nahe
to approach	sich nähern
neighbour	der Nachbar
to determine	bestimmen
limit	die Grenze
region	die Region, die Gegend
country	das Land
compatriot	der Landsmann

342

citizen	der Bürger
city	die Stadt
population	die Bevölkerung
to people	bevölkern
populous	volkreich
village	das Dorf
people	die Leute
province	die Provinz
provincial	provinziell
place	der Ort

Places   *Die Orte*

343

Africa	Afrika
African	afrikanisch
North America	Nordamerika
North American	nordamerikanisch
South America	Südamerika
South American	südamerikanisch
Central America	Mittelamerika
Central American	mittelamerikanisch

Australia	Australien
Australian	australisch

344

Europe	Europa
European	europäisch
Arctic	die Arktik
Antarctica	die Antarktik
Oceania	Ozeanien
Oceanian	ozeanisch
Asia	Asien
Asian	asiatisch
New Zealand	Neuseeland
New Zealander	der Neuseeländer, die Neuseeländerin

345

Spain	Spanien
Spanish	spanisch
Germany	Deutschland
German	deutsch
Italy	Italien
Italian	italienisch
Greece	Griechenland
Greek	griechisch
Russia	Rußland
Russian	russisch

346

Switzerland	die Schweiz
Swiss	schweizerisch
Holland	Holland
Dutch	holländisch
Portugal	Portugal
Portuguese	portugiesisch
Belgium	Belgien
Belgian	belgisch

125

Great Britain	Großbritannien
British Isles	die britischen Inseln

347

United Kingdom	das Vereinigte Königreich
British	britisch
England	England
English	englisch
Scotland	Schotland
Scottish	schottisch
Wales	Wales
Welsh	walisisch
Northern Ireland	Nordirland
Northern Irish	nordirisch

348

Ireland	Irland
Irish	irisch
France	Frankreich
French	französisch
Austria	Österreich
Austrian	österreichisch
Scandinavia	Skandinavien
Scandinavian	skandinavisch
Iceland	Island
Icelandic	isländisch

349

Greenland	Grönland
Greenlander	grönländisch
Sweden	Schweden
Swedish	schwedisch
Norway	Norwegen
Norwegian	norwegisch
Finland	Finland
Finnish	finnisch

Denmark	Dänemark
Danish	dänisch

350

Bavaria	Bayern
Bavarian	bayerisch
Saxony	Sachsen
Saxon	sächsisch
Alsace	das Elsaß
Alsatian	elsässisch
Lorraine	Lothringen

351

London	London
London *adj*	Londoner
Paris	Paris
Parisian	Pariser
Madrid	Madrid
Madrid *adj*	Madrider
Munich	München
Brunswick	Braunschweig
Cologne	Köln

352

Toulouse	Toulouse
Milan	Mailand
Lisbon	Lissabon
Bordeaux	Bordeaux
Lyons	Lyon
Bratislava	Preßburg
The Hague	den Haag (*also* der Haag)

353

Rome	Rom
Roman	römisch
Venice	Venedig
Venetian	venezianisch, der Venezianer

Naples	Neapel
Neapolitan	neapolitanisch, der Neapolitaner
Florence	Florenz
Florentine	florentinisch, der Florentiner
Turin	Turin

354

Hamburg	Hamburg
Hanover	Hannover
Basle	Basel
Vienna	Wien
Viennese	Wiener
Antwerp	Antwerpen
Berlin	Berlin
Berlin *adj*	Berliner
Geneva	Genf
Geneva *adj*	Genfer

355

Athens	Athen
Brussels	Brüssel
Strasbourg	Straßburg
Bruges	Brügge
Moscow	Moskau
Muscovite	Moskowiter
Warsaw	Warschau
Prague	Prag
Budapest	Budapest

356

Copenhagen	Kopenhagen
New York	New York
New York *adj*	New Yorker
Cairo	Kairo
Capetown	Kapstadt
Beijing	Peking

357
Poland	Polen
Polish	polnisch
Czech Republic	die Tschechische Republik
Czech	tschechisch
Slovakia	die Slowakei
Slovak	slowakisch
Slovenia	Slowenien
Slovene	slowenisch
Croatia	Kroatien
Croatian	kroatisch

358
Hungary	Ungarn
Hungarian	ungarisch
Bosnia	Bosnien
Bosnian	bosnisch
Serbia	Serbien
Serbian	serbisch
Albania	Albanien
Albanian	albanisch
Romania	Rumänien
Romanian	rumänisch

359
Bulgaria	Bulgarien
Bulgarian	bulgarisch
Macedonia	Mazedonien
Macedonian	mazedonisch
Moldova	Moldawien
Moldovan	moldauisch
Belarus	Weißrußland
Belorussian	weißrussisch
Ukraine	die Ukraine
Ukrainian	ukrainisch

360

Estonia	Estland
Estonian	estländisch
Latvia	Lettland
Latvian	lettisch
Lithuania	Lithauen
Lithuanian	lithauisch
Armenia	Armenien
Armenian	armenisch
Azerbaijan	Aserbaidschan
Azerbaijani	aserbaidschanisch

361

Georgia	Georgien
Georgian	georgisch
Siberia	Sibirien
Siberian	sibirisch
Turkey	die Türkei
Turkish	türkisch
Arabia	Arabien
Arab	arabisch
Morocco	Marokko
Moroccan	marokanisch

362

Egypt	Ägypten
Egyptian	ägyptisch
China	China
Chinese	chinesisch
India	Indien
Indian	indisch
Japan	Japan
Japanese	japanisch
Ghana	Ghana
Ghanaian	ghanaisch

363

Algeria	Algerien
Algerian	algerisch
Tunisia	Tunesien
Tunisian	tunesisch
South Africa	Südafrika
South African	südafrikanisch
Israel	Israel
Israeli	israelisch
Palestine	Palästina
Palestinian	palästinensisch

364

Castile	Kastilien
Castilian	kastilianisch
Andalusia	Andalusien
Andalusian	andalusisch
Catalonia	Katalonien
Catalan	katalonisch
Galicia	Galizien
Galician	galizisch
Basque Country	das Baskenland
Basque	baskisch

365

United States	die Vereinigten Staaten
North American	nordamerikanisch
Canada	Kanada
Canadian	kanadisch
Mexico	Mexico
Mexican	mexikanisch
Colombia	Kolumbien
Colombian	kolumbianisch
Peru	Peru
Peruvian	peruanisch

366

Brazil	Brasilien
Brazilian	brasilianisch
Chile	Chile
Chilean	chilenisch
Argentina	Argentinien
Argentinian	argentinisch
Uruguay	Uruguay
Uruguayan	uruguayisch
Bolivia	Bolivien
Bolivian	bolivianisch

367

Pyrenees	die Pyreneen
Alps	die Alpen
Atlas Mountains	das Atlasgebirge
Dolomites	die Dolomiten
Carpathians	die Karpaten
Andes	die Anden
Himalayas	der Himalaya
Mont Blanc	der Mont Blanc
Table Mountain	das Tafelgebirge
Everest	Mount Everest

368

Amazon	der Amazonas
Nile	der Nil
Rhine	der Rhein
Rhône	die Rhone
Tagus	der Tajo
Danube	die Donau
Thames	die Themse
Seine	die Seine
Loire	die Loire
Ebro	der Ebro

369

Atlantic	der Atlantik
Pacific	der Pazifik
Arctic	die Arktik
Indian	der Indische Ozean
Antarctic	die Antarktik
Mediterranean	das Mittelmeer
North Sea	die Nordsee
Black Sea	das Schwarze Meer
Red Sea	das Rote Meer
Caribbean	die Karibik

370

Baltic Sea	die Ostsee
English Channel	der Ärmelkanal
Bay of Biscay	die Biskaya
West Indies	die Westindischen Inseln
Canaries	die Kanarischen Inseln
The Philippines	die Philippinen
Balearic Islands	die Balearischen Inseln
Sicily	Sizilien
Sardinia	Sardinien
Corsica	Korsika

371

Corsican	korsisch
Rhodes	Rhodos
Crete	Kreta
Cretan	kretisch
Cyprus	Zypern
Cypriot	zypriotisch
Dardanelles	die Dardanellen
Bosphorus	der Bosporus
Scilly Isles	die Scillyinseln
Falkland Islands	die Falklandinseln

372
weights	die Gewichtsmaße *pl*
weight	das Gewicht
to weigh	wiegen
heavy	schwer
light	leicht
scales	die Wage *sing*
to measure	messen
measure	das Maß
to compare	vergleichen
comparison	der Vergleich

373
to contain	enthalten
contents	der Inhalt
metric system	das metrische System
metre	der Meter
centimetre	der Zentimeter
millimetre	der Millimeter
gram	das Gramm
kilogram	das Kilogramm
litre	der Liter
hectare	der Hektar

374
kilometre	der Kilometer
ton	die Tonne
inch	der Zoll
foot	der Fuß
mile	die Meile
arithmetic	das Rechnen
mathematics	die Mathematik
to calculate	berechnen

to count	zählen
number	die Zahl

375

figure	die Ziffer
zero	die Null
addition	die Addition
to add	addieren
subtraction	die Subtraktion
remainder	der Rest
equal	gleich
equality	die Gleichheit
to multiply	multiplizieren
product	das Produkt

376

to produce	produzieren
producer	der Produzent
to divide	dividieren, teilen
part	der Teil
fraction	der Bruch
half	die Hälfte
third	das Drittel
quarter	das Viertel
dozen	das Dutzend
double	doppelt

377

triple	dreifach
geometry	die Geometrie
algebra	die Algebra
space	der Raum
spacious	geräumig
parallel	parallel
perpendicular	vertikal
horizontal	horizontal

horizon	der Horizont
right angle	der rechte Winkel

378

triangle	das Dreieck
square	das Quadrat
curved	gebogen
straight	gerade
circumference	der Umfang
circle	der Kreis
centre	das Zentrum
diameter	der Durchmesser
problem	die Aufgabe
correct	richtig

379

incorrect	falsch
wrong	falsch
simple	einfach
to complicate	komplizieren
to demonstrate	demonstrieren
to solve	lösen
result	das Ergebnis
to result	ergeben
physics	die Physik
physical	physikalisch

380

matter	die Materie
pressure	der Druck
phenomenon	das Phänomen
strange	merkwürdig
movement	die Bewegung
to move	(sich) bewegen
mobile	beweglich
immobile	unbeweglich

electric	elektrisch
electricity	die Elektrizität

381

mechanics	die Mechanik
invent	erfinden
optics	die Optik
optical	optisch
microscope	das Mikroskop
lens	die Linse
to reflect	spiegeln
reflection	die Reflektion
chemistry	die Chemie
chemical	chemisch

382

biology	die Biologie
biological	biologisch
biologist	der Biologe
to research	untersuchen
researcher	der Forscher
element	das Element
oxygen	der Sauerstoff
hydrogen	der Wasserstoff
atom	das Atom
nucleus	der Kern

383

laboratory	das Labor
experiment	der Versuch, das Experiment
mixture	die Mischung
mixed	gemischt
to decompose	(sich) zersetzen
to compose	zusammensetzen
compound	die Verbindung
rare	selten

| science | die Wissenschaft |
| scientific | wissenschaftlich |

384
scientist	der Wissenschaftler
knowledge	das Wissen
to know (something)	wissen
to know (person)	kennen
wisdom	die Weisheit
wise	weise
sage	der Weise
to be ignorant of	nichts wissen von
experience	die Erfahrung
inexperience	der Erfahrungsmangel

Communications *die Kommunikation*

385
telegraph	der Telegraph
telegram	das Telegramm
to telegraph	telegrapghieren
telex	das Telex
telephone	das Telefon
to telephone	telefonieren, anrufen
telephonist	der Telefonist, die Telefonistin
call	der Anruf
receiver	der Hörer
mouthpiece	die Sprechmuschel

386
telephone booth	die Telefonzelle
telephone exchange	die Telefonzentrale
telephone directory	das Telefonbuch
telephone subscriber	der Telefonbesitzer
answerphone	der Anrufbeantworter
to hang up	aufhängen

engaged	besetzt
to dial	wählen
radiotelephone	das Funktelefon
videophone	das Bildtelefon

387

fax	das Fax
to fax	faxen
modem	das Modem
electronic mail	die elektronische Post
information technology	die Informationstechnologie
microelectronics	die Mikroelektronik
screen	der Bildschirm
keyboard	die Tastatur
key	die Taste
mouse	die Maus

388

computer	der Computer
computer language	die Computersprache
computer literate	computerkundig
computer scientist	der Informatiker, die Informatikerin
computer game	das Computerspiel
computer animation	die Computeranimation
computer aided design	die rechnergestützte Konstruktion
computerese	das Computerchinesisch
to computerise	auf Computer umstellen
computerisation	die Umstellung auf Computer

389

to program	programmieren
programmer	der Programmierer
systems analyst	der Systemanalytiker
wordprocessor	das Textverarbeitungsgerät

memory	der Speicher
disk drive	das Diskettenlaufwerk, das Plattenlaufwerk
software	die Software
hardware	die Hardware
shareware	die Shareware
cursor	der Cursor

390
menu	das Menü
to store	speichern
file	die Datei
to file	ablegen
data	die Daten
database	die Datenbank
desktop publishing	das Desktop Publishing
to lay out	layouten
silicon	das Silikon
silicon chip	der Silikonchip

391
user-friendly	anwenderfreundlich
laser printer	der Laserdrucker
bubble jet printer	der Bubble-Jet-Drucker
scanner	der Scanner
circuit	der Kreislauf
fibreoptics	die Faseroptik
machine translation	die Maschinenübersetzung
network	das Netz
networking	die Vernetzung
information superhighway	der Informations-Superhighway

The Arts and Entertainment
Die schönen Künste und die Unterhaltung

392

painting	die Malerei
painter	der Maler, die Malerin
to paint	malen
picturesque	malerisch
artist	der Künstler, die Künstlerin
museum	das Museum
engraving	die Radierung
to engrave	radieren
print	der Druck
background	der Hintergrund

393

foreground	der Vordergrund
still life	das Stilleben
drawing	die Zeichnung
to draw	zeichnen
draughtsman	der Zeichner
outline	der Umriß
to imitate	imitieren
imitation	die Imitation
abstract	abstrakt
innovative	innovativ

394

to innovate	innovieren
resemblance	die Ähnlichkeit
similar	ähnlich
forgery	die Fälschung
forger	der Fälscher, die Fälscherin
auction	die Versteigerung, die Auktion
to bid	bieten

lot	die Partie
reserve price	der Mindestpreis
exhibition	die Ausstellung

395

antique	die Antiquität
antique dealer	der Antiquitätenhändler
art dealer	der Kunsthändler
palette	die Palette
brush	der Pinsel
easel	die Staffelei
colour	die Farbe
to colour	färben
coloured	gefärbt
dull	trüb

396

multicoloured	vielfarbig
contrast	der Gegensatz
to contrast	kontrastieren
white	weiß
black	schwarz
light blue	hellblau
dark green	dunkelgrün
yellow	gelb
brown	braun
chestnut	kastanienbraun

397

pink	rosa
red	rot
violet	violett
mauve	lila
purple	purpurfarben
gilt	vergoldet
to gild	vergolden

grey	grau
patron	der Mäzen
patronage	die Förderung

398

patronise	fördern
oils	das Ölbild
watercolour	das Aquarrell
fresco	das Fresko
triptych	das Triptychon
cartoon	der Comic
the Renaissance	die Renaissance
Renaissance art	die Renaissancekunst
crayon	der Wachsmalkreide, die Ölkreide
canvas	die Leinwand

399

gallery	die Gallerie
tone	der Ton
landscape	die Landschaft
portrait	das Porträt
portraitist	der Porträtmaler, die Porträtmalerin
miniature	die Miniatur
miniaturist	der Miniaturenmaler, die Miniaturenmalerin
landscape painter	der Landschaftsmaler, die Landschaftsmalerin
impressionism	der Impressionismus
impressionist	impressionistisch

400

surrealism	der Surrealismus
surrealist	surreaslistisch
cubism	der Kubismus
cubist	kubistisch
symbol	das Symbol

to symbolise	symbolisieren
symbolic	symbolisch
sculpture	die Plastik
sculptor	der Bildhauer, die Bildhauerin
workshop	das Atelier

401

to carve	schnitzen
model	das Modell
statue	die Statue
bust	die Büste
group	die Gruppe
chisel	der Meißel
cast	der Guß
shape	die Form
to shape	formen
architecture	die Architektur

402

architect	der Architekt
vault	das Gewölbe
dome	die Kuppel
pillar	die Säule
arch	der Bogen
tower	der Turm
scaffolding	das Gerüst
arch	der Bogen
column	die Säule
plinth	die Fußleiste

403

nave	das Schiff
cathedral	der Dom
cathedral city	die Domstadt
apse	die Apsis
stained glass	das Kirchenfensterglas

transept	das Querschiff
flying buttress	das Strebewerk
font	das Taufbecken
crypt	die Krypta
basilica	die Basilika

404

Gothic	gothisch
Romanesque	romanisch
Baroque	barock
mosque	die Moschee
minaret	das Minarett
synagogue	die Synagoge
pagoda	die Pagode
mausoleum	das Mausoleum
pyramid	die Pyramide
Sphinx	die Sphynx

405

temple	der Tempel
Corinthian	korynthisch
Ionian	ionisch
Doric	dorisch
forum	das Forum
amphitheatre	das Amphitheater
aqueduct	das Aquädukt
dolmen	der Dolmen
menhir	der Menhir
cave painting	die Höhlenmalerei

406

illiterate (person)	der Analphabet
literate	lesekundig
oral tradition	die mündliche Tradition
ballad	die Ballade
saga	die Saga

tradition	die Tradition
story	die Geschichte
storyteller	der Geschichtenerzähler
narrative	die Erzählung
to learn by heart	auswendig lernen

407

literature	die Literatur
papyrus	der Papyrus
parchment	das Pergament
alphabet	das Alpbabet
character	die Person
author	der Autor
writer	der Schriftsteller
editor	der Herausgeber
edition	die Ausgabe
copyright	das Urheberrecht

408

style	der Stil
reader	der Leser, die Leserin
biography	die Biographie
biographer	der Biographieautor, die Biographieautorin
biographical	biographisch
autobiography	die Autobiographie
autobiographical	autobiographisch
fiction	die Belletristik
fictional	fiktiv
science fiction	die Science Fictions

409

novel	der Roman
novelist	der Romanautor, die Romanautorin
publisher	der Verleger, die Verlegerin
royalties	die Tandiemen

bookshop	die Buchhandlung
bookseller	der Buchhändler, die Buchhändlerin
encyclopaedia	die Enzyklopädie
encyclopaedic	enzyklopädisch
paperback	das Taschenbuch
poetry	die Poesie

410

poet	der Dichter, die Dichterin
poetic	poetisch
rhyme	der Reim
to rhyme	sich reimen
metre	das Metrum
stanza	der Vers
sonnet	das Sonett
assonance	die Assonanz
syllable	die Silbe
nursery rhyme	der Kinderreim

411

fairy tale	das Märchen
Cinderella	Aschenputtel
Red Riding Hood	Rotkäppchen
Snow White	Schneewittchen
dwarf	der Zwerg
goblin	der Kobold
gnome	der Gnom
elf	die Elfe
Sleeping Beauty	Dornröschen
Snow Queen	die Schneekönigin

412

Puss in Boots	der Gestiefelte Kater
Bluebeard	Blaubart
witch	die Hexe
wizard	der Hexer

spell	der Zauberspruch
to cast a spell	verwünschen
magician	der Zauberer
magic	die Zauberei
magical	magisch
mermaid	die Meerjungfrau

413

mythology	die Mythologie
Homer	Homer
Homeric	homerisch
Iliad	die Ilias
Odyssey	die Odyssee
Odysseus	Odysseus
Trojan	trojanisch
Trojan horse	das trojanische Pferd
Achilles	Achilles
Achilles heel	die Achillesferse

414

Cyclops	der Zyklop
Atlantis	Atlantis
Romulus	Romulus
Hercules	Herkules
Herculean	herkulisch
The Arabian Nights	Tausendundeine Nacht
Armageddon	der Armageddon
Valhalla	die Walhalla
Thor	Thor
rune	die Rune

415

masterpiece	das Meisterwerk
music	die Musik
musician	der Musiker, die Musikerin
to play (an instrument)	spielen

composer	der Komponist, die Komponistin
orchestra	das Orchester
symphony	die Symphonie
aria	die Arie
overture	die Ouvertüre
march	der Marsch

416

soft	sanft
stringed instrument	das Seiteninstrument
wind instrument	das Blasinstrument
brass instrument	das Blechblasinstrument
piano	das Piano, das Klavier
pianist	der Pianist
organ	die Orgel
organist	der Organist
harmony	die Harmonie
flute	die Querflöte

417

to blow	blasen
bagpipes	der Dudelsack
cornet	das Horn
violin	die Violine
auditorium	die Zuhörer *pl*
score	die Partitur
opera	die Oper
tenor	der Tenor
soprano	der Sopran
baritone	der Bariton

418

bass	der Baß
conductor	der Dirigent, die Dirigentin
instrumentalist	der Instrumentalist, die Instrumentalistin

rehearsal	die Probe
violin	die Violine, die Geige
viola	die Bratsche
violinist	der Violinist, die Violinistin
cello	das Cello
bow	der Bogen
guitar	die Gitarre

419

to strum	herumklimpern
harp	die Harpe
flute	die Querflöte
oboe	die Oboe
clarinet	die Klarinette
bassoon	das Fagott
trumpet	die Trompete
trombone	die Posaune
French horn	das Waldhorn
tuba	die Tuba

420

songbook	das Liederbuch
singing	der Gesang
to sing	singen
to enchant	bezaubern
enchanting, delightful	bezaubernd
spell, charm	der Zauber
singer	der Sänger, die Sängerin
choir	der Chor
to accompany	begleiten
accompaniment	die Begleitung

421

song	das Lied
refrain	der Refrain
concert	das Konzert

to syncopate	synkopieren
jazz	der Jazz
beat	der Beat
saxophone	das Saxophon
rock music	die Rockmusik
rock star	der Rockstar
drums	das Schlagzeug

422

synthesiser	der Synthesizer
folk music	die Volksmusik
mandolin	die Mandoline
ocarina	die Okarina
drum	die Trommel
accordion	das Akordeon
xylophone	das Xylophon
zither	die Zither
concertina	die Concertina

423

dance, dancing	der Tanz
to dance	tanzen
ball, dance	der Ball
dancer	der Tänzer, die Tänzerin
theatre	das Theater
theatrical	theatralisch
mask	die Maske
box office	die Kasse
seat, place	der Platz
stalls	der Sperrsitz
box (theatre)	die Loge

424

pit	das Parkett
stage	die Bühne
scene	die Szene

act	der Akt
interval	die Pause
scenery	das Bühnenbild
curtain	der Vorhang
play	das Theaterstück
playwright	der Theaterautor
character	die Person

425

tragedy	die Tragödie
comedy	die Komödie
actor	der Schauspieler
actress	die Schauspielerin
to play a role	eine Rolle spielen
to be word-perfect	seine Rolle genau kennen
costume	das Kostüm
lighting	die Belleuchtung
dénouement	die Auflösung
to stage, represent	auf die Bühne bringen, darstellen

426

performance	die Vorführung
flop	der Flop
to flop	durchfallen
debut, first performance	die Premiere
trapdoor	die Versenkung
to be a success	ein Erfolg sein
audience	das Publikum
spectator	der Zuschauer
applause	der Aplaus
whistling, hissing	die Pfiffe *pl*, die Buhrufe *pl*

427

| cinema | das Kino |
| screen | die Leinwand |

to dub	synchronisieren
to subtitle	mit Untertiteln versehen
subtitle	der Untertitel
sequel	die Folge
director	der Regisseur
producer	der Produzent
to censor	zensieren
censorship	die Zensur

428

to whistle, hiss	pfeifen, ausbuhen
amusements	die Unterhaltung
playground	der Spielplatz
to enjoy oneself	sich unterhalten
entertaining	unterhaltsam
amusing	vergnüglich
pastime	der Zeitvertreib
rest	die Ruhe
to rest	ruhen
weariness	die Müdigkeit

429

to get tired	ermüden
tired	müde
to be bored	sich langweilen
boring	langweilig
fair	das Straßenfest, die Kirchweih
festival	das Fest
crowd	die Menge
to assemble	zusammensetzen
circus	der Zirkus
trapeze	das Trapez

430

trapeze artist	der Trapezkünstler, die Trapezkünst-lerin

153

tightrope	das Seil
tightrope walker	der Seiltänzer, die Seiltänzerin
acrobat	der Akrobat, die Akrobatin
acrobatic	akrobatisch
acrobatics	die Akrobatik
clown	der Clown
joke	der Witz
lottery	die Lotterie
to be lucky	Glück haben

431

luck	das Glück
swing	die Schaukel
to swing (oneself)	schaukeln
seesaw	die Wippe
roundabout	das Karusell
game	das Spiel
to play	spielen
player	der Spieler
toy	das Spielzeug
match	das Match

432

to win	gewinnen
to lose	verlieren
to draw	zeichnen
to cheat	mogeln
deceit	die Täuschung
meeting	das Treffen
to meet	sich treffen
to join	sich zusammenschließen
party	die Gruppe

433

to visit	besuchen
visit	der Besuch

playing cards	die Spielkarten
to deal	handeln
to shuffle	mischen
suit	der Satz
billiards	Billard
cue	das Queue
cannon	die Karambolage
spin	der Effekt

434

chess	das Schach
piece	die Figur
pawn	der Bauer
rook	der Turm
bishop	der Läufer
knight	der Springer
chessboard	das Schachbrett
draughts	das Damespiel
dice	die Würfel *pl*
jigsaw	das Puzzle

Sport   *Der Sport*

435

swimming	das Schwimmen
to swim	schwimmen
swimmer	der Schwimmer, die Schwimmerin
breaststroke	das Brustschwimmen
crawl	das Kraulen
backstroke	das Rückenschwimmen
butterfly	der Delphinstil
lifeguard	der Bademeister
to dive	tauchen

436

high diving	das Turmspringen

to row	rudern
rower	der Ruderer
oar	das Ruder
canoe	das Kanu
canoeing	das Kanufahren
canoeist	der Kanufahrer
paddle	das Paddel
skate	der Schlittschuh
to skate	Schlittschuh fahren

437

figure skating	der Eistanz
rollerskates	die Rollschuhe
skateboard	das Skateboard
amateur	der Amateur
bet	die Wette
to bet	wetten
odds	die Chancen
ball	der Ball
football (sport)	der Fußball

438

football	der Fußball
footballer	der Fußballer
football pools	die Fußballwetten, das Fußballtoto
referee	der Schiedsrichter
penalty	die Strafe
corner	die Ecke
offside	das Abseits
forward	der Stürmer
defender	der Verteidiger
midfielder	der Mittelstürmer

439

winger	der (Links/Rechts-)Außen
to score	ein Tor schießen

to shoot	schießen
to dribble	dribbeln
goal	das Tor
goalpost	der Torpfosten
goalkeeper	der Torhüter
goalscorer	der Torschütze
goal-kick	der Torschuß
team	die Mannschaft

440
league	die Liga
trophy	die Trophäe
knockout	der Ausschußwettbewerb
rugby	das Rugby
to tackle	angreifen
scrum	das Gedränge
scrum-half	der Gedrängehalbspieler
fly-half	der Öffnungshalbspieler
prop	der Pfosten
fullback	der Verteidiger

441
tennis	das Tennis
lawn tennis	das Rasentennisspiel
tennis player	der Tennisspieler, die Tennisspielerin
set	der Satz
volley	der Flugball
to serve	anschlagen
table tennis	das Tischtennis
racket	der Schläger
boxing	das Boxen

442
boxer	der Boxer
wrestling	das Ringen
champion	der Champion

fencing	das Fechten
fencer	der Fechter, die Fechterin
foil	Florettfechten
gymnast	der Turner, die Turnerin
gymnastics	das Turnen
somersault	die Rolle
cycling	das Radfahren

443

cyclist	der Radfahrer, die Radfahrerin
mountain bicycle	das Mountainbike
time trial	der Zeitkampf
stage	das Stadium
yellow jersey	das gelbe Trikot
horseriding	das Reiten
showjumping	das Kunstspringen
dressage	die Dressur
polo	das Polo
horseman	der Reiter, die Reiterin

444

grandstand	die Tribüne
racecourse	die Rennbahn
race	das Rennen
to run	rennen
bullfight	der Stierkampf
bull fighter	der Torero
motor racing	das Motorrennen
scrambling	das Motocross
hockey	das Hockey
bowls	das Kegeln

445

stadium	das Stadium
high jump	der Hochsprung
record	der Rekord

long jump	der Weitsprung
triple jump	der Dreisprung
pole vault	der Stabhochsprung
long-distance runner	der Langstreckenläufer, die Langstreckenläuferin
lap	der Sprung
marathon	der Marathon
training	das Training

446

athletics	die Leichtathletik
athlete	der Leichtathlet, die Leichtathletin
sprinter	der Sprinter, die Sprinterin
sprint	der Sprint
to sprint	sprinten
shotput	das Kugelstoßen

447

discus	der Diskuswurf
hammer	das Hammerwerfen
relay race	der Staffellauf
baton	der Tambourstock
Olympics	die Olympiade *sing*
triathlon	der Triathlon
triathlete	der Triathlet, die Triathletin
decathlon	der Dekathlon
decathlete	der Deklathlete, die Deklathletin
pentathlon	der Pentathlon

448

pentathlete	der Pentathlet, die Pentathletin
mountaineering	das Bergsteigen
mountaineer	der Bergsteiger, die Bergsteigerin
rock climbing	das Felsklettern
rock climber	der Felskletterer, die Felsklettererin

ice-axe	der Eispickel
skiing	das Skifahren
to ski	Ski fahren
ski	der Ski
cross-country skiing	der Langlauf

449
ski-lift	der Skilift
skier	der Skifahrer, die Skifahrerin
ski-stick	der Skistock
ski-jump	das Skispringen
snowshoes	Schneeschuhe
ice hockey	das Eishockey
puck	der Puck
water skiing	der Wasserski
outboard motor	der Außenmotor

450
slalom	der Slalom
to abseil	sich abseilen
fish	der Fisch
angling	das Angeln
fishing rod	die Angelrute
reel	die Leine
bait	der Köder
to bait	ködern
hook	der Haken
fly fishing	das Fliegenfischen

Food and Drink Essen und Trinken

451
food	das Essen
provisions	die Lebensmittel
to nourish	ernähren

appetite	der Appetit
snack	der Imbiß
to have a snack	einen Imbiß einnehmen
hunger	der Hunger
hungry	hungrig
thirst	der Durst
thirsty	durstig

452

to be hungry	Hunger haben
to be thirsty	Durst haben
sweet	süß
to have a sweet tooth	eine Schwäche für Süßes haben
sugar	der Zucker
sugary	zuckrig
tasteless	geschmacklos
bitter	bitter
milk	die Milch
to pasteurise	pasteurisieren

453

skimmed milk	die entrahmte Milch
whole milk	die Vollmilch
cream	die Sahne
butter	die Butter
buttermilk	die Buttermilch
cheese	der Käse
egg	das Ei
yolk	das Eigelb
egg white	das Eiweiß
shell	die Schale

454

soft boiled egg	das weichgekochte Ei
scrambled eggs	die Rühreier

omelette	das Omelette
bread	das Brot
brown bread	das Graubrot. das Schwarzbrot
sliced bread	das in Scheiben geschnittene Brot
loaf	der Leib
roll	das Brötchen
crumb	der Krümel, die Krume
crust	die Kruste

455

health foods	die Reformkost
organically grown	aus organischem Anbau
vegetarian	der Vegetarier, die Vegetarierin
fibre	der Ballaststoff
wholemeal bread	das Vollkornbrot
rye bread	das Roggenbrot
to slim	abnehmen
lentil	die Linse
margarine	die Margarine
polyunsaturated	mehrfach ungesättigt

456

fast food	das Fast Food
hamburger	der Hamburger
hot dog	das Hot Dog
pizza	die Pizza
fat	das Fett
fatty food	das fettreiche Essen
frozen food	die Tiefkühlnahrung
french fries	die Pommes frites *pl*
crisps	die Chips
confectionery	die Süßwaren *pl*

457

| vegetable | das Gemüse |
| carrot | die Karottte |

broccoli	der Broccoli
onion	die Zwiebel
celery	der Sellerie
radish	das Radieschen
spinach	der Spinat
asparagus	der Spargel
cucumber	die Gurke
gherkin	das Cornichon

458
lettuce	der Salat
tomato	die Tomate
pea	die Erbse
chickpea	die Kichererbse
bean	die Bohne
French bean	die grüne Bohne
haricot bean	die weiße Bohne
cauliflower	der Blumenkohl
Brussels sprout	der Rosenkohl
aubergine	die Aubergine

459
salad	der Salat
mixed salad	der gemischte Salat
corn	der Mais
beetroot	die rote Beete
green pepper	der grüne Paprika
mashed potato	das Kartoffelpüree
garlic	der Knoblauch
squash	der Squash
courgette	die Zucchini
marrow	der Markkürbis

460
tomato	die Tomate
mushroom	der Champignon

condiment	das Würzmittel
spice	das Gewürz
coriander	der Koriander
mustard	der Senf
nutmeg	Muskatnuß
cinnamon	der Zimt
turmeric	der Kurkuma
saffron	der Safran

461

soup	die Suppe
soup tureen	die Suppenterrine
broth	die Brühe
beef	das Rindfleisch
veal	das Kalbfleisch
steak	das Steak
rare	blutig
well done	durch
sauce	die Soße
gravy	die Bratensoße

462

cutlet	das Kotelett
ham	der Schinken
bacon	der Speck
sausage	die Wurst
pepperoni	die Pepperoni
blood sausage	die Blutwurst
raw	roh
soft	weich
hard	hart
stew	der Eintopf

463

| tripe | die Kutteln *pl* |
| cooking | das Kochen |

cook	der Koch, die Köchin
to cook	kochen
to roast	rösten
roast	der Braten
to stew	schmoren
to slice	in Scheiben schneiden
slice	die Scheibe
to fry	braten

464

fried	gebraten
chicken	das Hähnchen
breast	die Brust
leg	der Schlegel
ham	der Schinken
to cure	pökeln
to smoke (food)	räuchern
lamb	das Lammfleisch
pork	das Schweinefleisch
veal	das Kalbfleisch

465

to grill	grillen
to barbecue	grillen
barbecue	der Holzkohlengrill
to bake	backen
breaded	paniert
scampi	die Scampi *pl*
to stuff	füllen
spit	der Spieß
suckling pig	das Ferkel
shank (lamb)	die (Lamms-)Haxe

466

fish	der Fisch
haddock	der Schellfisch

mussel	die Mießmuschel
mullet	die Meerbarbe
mackerel	die Makrele
clam	die Muschel
sole	die Seezunge
tuna	der Thunfisch
salad	der Salat
oil	das Öl

467
vinegar	der Essig
sour	sauer
cruet	Essig und Öl
salt	das Salz
saltcellar	der Salzstreuer
to salt	salzen
pepper	der Pfeffer
pepperpot	der Pfefferstreuer
mustard	der Senf
mayonnaise	die Mayonnaise

468
jam	die Konfitüre
marmalade	die Marmelade
cake	der Kuchen
pastry-cook	der Konditor
dough	der Teig
dessert	der Nachtisch
pancake	der Pfannkuchen
rice pudding	der Reispudding
custard	die Eierkrem
roast apple	der Bratapfel

469
caramel cream	die Creme Caramel
ice cream	das Speiseeis

chocolate	die Schokolade
chocolate mousse	die Mousse au Chocolat
fritters	die Beignets
sponge cake	der Biskuitkuchen
fruit salad	der Obstsalat
whipped cream	die Schlagsahne
cheese cake	der Käsekuchen
lemon meringue	die Zitronenbaiserkuchen

470

pudding	die Süßspeise
biscuit	das Plätzchen
baby food	die Babynahrung
flour	das Mehl
self-raising flour	das Mehl mit Backpulver
yeast	die Hefe
baking soda	Natron
lard	das Schmalz
oil	das Öl
sunflower oil	das Sonnenblumenöl

471

olive oil	das Olivenöl
rice	der Reis
yoghurt	der Joghurt
doughnut	der Krapfen, der Berliner
apple compote	das Apfelmuß
sandwich	das Sandwich, das belegte Brot
spaghetti	die Spaghetti
cake	der Kuchen
noodle	die Nudel
frog legs	die Froschschenkel

472

restaurant	das Restaurant
menu	die Speisekarte

starter	die Vorspeise
first course	der erste Gang
waitress	die Bedienung
waiter	der Kellner, der Ober
drink	das Getränk
to drink	trinken
to sip	nippen
to gulp	in großen Zügen trinken

473

to empty	leeren
empty	leer
nonalcoholic drink	das alkoholfreie Getränk
wine	der Wein
red wine	der Rotwein
rosé wine	der Roséwein
vintage	der Jahrgang
beer	das Bier
water	das Wasser
drinking water	das Trinkwasser

474

milkshake	der Milkshake
tonic	das Stärkungsmittel
juice	der Saft
soft drink	das Erfrischungsgetränk
sherry	der Sherry
dry	trocken
sherbet	das Sorbet
lemonade	die Limonade
fizzy	kohlensäurehaltig
to uncork	entkorken

475

corkscrew	der Korkenzieher
liqueur	der Likör

spirits	die alkoholischen Getränke
cognac	der Cognac
tonic water	das Tonicwasser
orange drink	das Orangengetränk
mineral water	das Mineralwasser
cappuccino	der Cappucino
tea	der Tee
camomile tea	der Kamillentee

476

lemon tea	der Zitronentee
coffee	der Kaffee
coffee with milk	der Kaffee mit Milch
decaffeinated coffee	der entkoffeinierte Kaffee
iced coffee	der Eiskaffee
instant coffee	der Instantkaffee
soda	das Sodawasser
whisky	der Whisky
canned beer	das Dosenbier
bottled beer	das Flaschenbier

477

cider	der Cidre, der Apfelwein
champagne	der Champagner, der Sekt
vermouth	der Wermut
vodka	der Wodka
rum	der Rum
Irish coffee	der Irish Coffee
anise	der Anis
brandy	der Weinbrand
cherry brandy	der Kirschlikör
applejack	der Apfelbranntwein

478
to travel	reisen
traveller	der Reisende
travel agency	das Reisebüro
travel agent	der Reisekaufmann
package holiday	der Pauschalurlaub
tourist	der Tourist, die Touristin
tourist season	die Fremdenverkehrssaison
hotel	das Hotel
hotelier	der Hotelier
reception	die Rezeption

479
information desk	der Informationsschalter
lobby	das Foyer
service	der Service
to book in advance	im voraus buchen
vacant	frei
bill	die Rechnung
tip	das Trinkgeld
hostel	die Herberge
youth hostel	die Jugendherberge
boarding house	die Pension

480
camping	das Zelten, das Camping
campsite	der Zeltplatz
to go camping	zelten gehen
camp-chair	der Klappstuhl
camping-van	der Campingbus
air mattress	die Luftmatratze
bottle-opener	der Flaschenöffner

camp bed	das Klappbett
tin-opener	der Dosenöffner

481

campfire	das Lagerfeuer
flashlight	die Taschenlampe
fly sheet	das Flugblatt
impermeable ground	wasserdichter Boden
ground sheet	die Bodenabdeckung
guy line	die Zeltleine
mallet	der Holzhammer
shelter	der Unterschlupf
to take shelter	Unterschlupf suchen
to get wet	naß werden

482

sleeping bag	der Schlafsack
to sleep out	im Freien schlafen
tent	das Zelt
tent peg	der Hering
tent pole	die Zeltstange
thermos flask	die Thermosflasche
caravan	der Caravan
to go caravaning	im Caravan reisen
to live rough	auf der Straße leben
tramp	der Landstreicher, der Stadtstreicher

483

self-catering apartment	die Ferienwohnung
day-tripper	der Tagesausflügler
trip	der Ausflug
railway	die Eisenbahn
platform	der Bahnsteig
to derail	entgleisen
derailment	die Entgleisung

to collide	zusammenstoßen
collision	die Kollision, der Zusammenstoß
accident	der Unfall

484

timetable	der Fahrplan
guidebook	der Führer
train	der Zug
express train	der Expreß
through train	der Direktzug
to arrive	ankommen
arrival	die Ankunft
to leave	abfahren
departure	die Abfahrt
departure board	der Abfahrtsfahrplan

485

underground (rail)	die U-Bahn
diesel	der Diesel
steam	der Dampf
corridor	der Korridor
to alight	aussteigen
halt	der Stopp
compartment	das Abteil
tunnel	das Tunnel
viaduct	das Viadukt
cutting	der Durchstich

486

railway network	der Bahnnetz
railhead	der Kopfbahnhof
railtrack	das Bahngleis
railworker	der Bahnarbeiter
stationmaster	der Stationsvorsteher
waiting room	der Wartesaal
single ticket	die Einzelkarte

return ticket	die Rückkarte
to examine	prüfen
ticket inspector	der Fahrkartenkontrolleur

487

guard	die Wache
engine driver	der Zugführer
signalman	der Bahnwärter
locomotive	die Lokomotive
carriage	der Wagen
sleeping car	der Schlafwagen
dining car	der Speisewagen
luggage	das Gepäck
to check in	anmelden
left luggage	die Gepäckaufbewahrung

488

trunk	die Truhe
case	der Koffer
rucksack	der Rucksack
stop	das Stoppsignal
to stop	anhalten
stay	der Aufenthalt
customs	der Zoll
customs officer	der Zollbeamte
examination	die Prüfung
to examine	prüfen

489

duty	der Zoll
tax	die Steuer
to tax	besteuern
declare	anmelden
duty-free	zollfrei
passport	der Paß
identity card	der Personalausweis

bus	der Bus
taxi	das Taxi
taxi driver	der Taxifahrer, die Taxifahrerin

490

driving licence	der Führerschein
to drive	fahren
motor car	das Auto
motoring	der Automobilismus
motorist	der Fahrer
to hire	mieten
trailer	der Anhänger
to give someone a lift	jemanden mitnehmen
hitchhiker	der Anhalter
to hitchhike	per Anhalter fahren

491

hitchhiking	das Fahren per Anhalter
sharp bend	die scharfe Kurve
to skid	schleudern
door (vehicle)	die Tür
window (vehicle)	das Fenster
to park	parken
to slow down	langsamer werden
to accelerate	beschleunigen
to start up	starten
to overtake	überholen

492

aerial	die Antenne
air filter	der Luftfilter
alternator	der Drehstromgenerator
antifreeze	das Frostschutzmittel
gearbox	die Gangschaltung
axle	die Achse
battery	die Batterie

flat	leer
bonnet	die Kühlerhaube
boot	der Kofferraum

493

brake fluid	die Bremsflüssigkeit
brake	die Bremse
to brake	bremsen
bumper	die Stoßstange
carburettor	der Vergaser
child seat	der Kindersitz
choke	der Choke
clutch	die Kupplung
cylinder	der Zylinder
horsepower	die Pferdestärke

494

disc brake	die Scheibenbremse
distributor	der Verteiler
dynamo	die Lichtmaschine
dynamic	dynamisch
engine	der Motor
exhaust	der Auspuff
fan belt	der Keilriemen
fuel gauge	die Benzinanzeige
fuel pump	die Benzinpumpe
fuse	die Sicherung

495

gear lever	der Ganghebel
generator	der Generator
to generate	generieren
alternating current	Wechselstrom
hand brake	die Handbremse
hazard lights	die Warnblinkanlage
horn	die Hupe

ignition	die Zündung
ignition key	der Zündschlüssel
indicator	der Blinker

496

jack	der Wagenheber
silencer	der Schalldämpfer
number plate	das Nummernschild
oil filter	der Ölfilter
points	die Anschlüsse
rear view mirror	das Rückfenster
reflector	das Katzenauge
reverse light	das Rücklicht
roof-rack	der Dachgepäckträger
seat	der Platz

497

seat-belt	der Sicherheitsgurt
shock absorber	der Stoßdämpfer
socket set	das Steckschlüsselset
spanner	der Schraubenschlüssel
spare part	das Ersatzteil
spark plug	die Zündkerze
speedometer	die Geschwindigkeitsanzeige
starter motor	der Anlasser
steering wheel	das Lenkrad
sun roof	das Schiebedach

498

suspension	die Federung
towbar	die Abschleppstange
transmission	die Übersetzung
tyre	der Reifen
wheel	das Rad
windscreen	die Windschutzscheibe
wipers	die Scheibenwischer

wrench	der Schraubenschlüssel
air bag	der Airbag
four-wheel drive	der Vierradantrieb

499

motorbike	das Motorrad
helmet	der Helm
bicycle	das Fahrrad
racing cycle	das Rennrad
pedal	das Pedal
to pedal	die Pedale treten
tube	der Schlauch
to puncture	beschädigt werden
chain	die Kette
pannier bag	die Radtasche

500

ship	das Schiff
boat	das Boot, das Schiff
sail	das Segel
to embark	an Bord gehen
to disembark	von Bord gehen
on board	an Bord
disembarkment	die Ausschiffung
to tow	tauen
tug	der Schlepper
crossing	die Überquerung

501

to cross	überqueren
passage	die Überfahrt
passenger	der Passagier
cabin	die Kabine
deck	das Deck
mast	der Mast
pilot	der Pilot

rudder	das Steuer
crew	die Mannschaft
anchor	der Anker

502

to cast anchor	Anker werfen
anchorage	die Verankerung
cargo	die Ladung
to sink	sinken
sinking	das Sinken
shipwreck	das Schiffswrack
signal	das Signal
to signal	Signal geben
lighthouse	der Leuchtturm
port	der Hafen

503

quay	der Kai
oil tanker	der Öltanker
to launch	vom Stapel lassen
salvage	die Bergung
to salvage	bergen
free on board	frei Bord
waybill	der Frachtbrief
hovercraft	das Hovercraft
hoverport	der Hovercraft-Hafen

504

stern	das Heck
bows	die Knoten
prow	der Bug
starboard	das Steuerbord
port	der Hafen
keel	der Kiel
figurehead	die Bugfigur
funnel	der Schornstein

| rigging | die Takelage |
| sail | das Segel |

505

raft	das Floß
galley	die Galeere
clipper	der Schnellsegler
schooner	der Schoner
whaler	der Walfänger
trawler	der Trawler
to trawl	mit Schleppnetz fischen
factory ship	das Fabrikschiff

506

hydrofoil	das Luftkissenboot
powerboat	das schnelle Motorboot
dinghy	das Beiboot
pontoon	der Ponton
liferaft	das Rettungsboot
aqualung	die Taucherlunge
diver	der Taucher, die Taucherin
navigation	die Steuerung
to navigate	steuern
to weigh anchor	die Anker lichten

507

balloon	der Ballon
airship	der Zeppelin
aviation	die Luftfahrt
airplane	das Flugzeug
flying boat	das Flugboot
airport	der Flughafen
air terminal	das Flughafenabfertigungsgebäude
passenger	der Passagier
business class	die Business Class
tourist class	die Tourist Class

508

farewell	die Verabschidung
air hostess	die Stewardess
to land	landen
forced landing	die Notlandung
to take off	abheben
takeoff	der Start
seatbelt	der Sicherheitsgurt
to fly	fliegen
propeller	der Propeller
pilot	der Pilot

509

autopilot	der Autopilot
black box	die Black Box
runway	die Startbahn, die Landebahn
undercarriage	das Fahrwerk
sound barrier	die Schallgrenze
to crash	abstürzen
glider	das Segelflugzeug
to glide	gleiten
hang-glider	der Drachensegler
autogyro	das Drehflügelflugzeug

Appendix

Days of the week	*Die Tage der Woche*
Monday	Montag
Tuesday	Dienstag
Wednesday	Mittwoch
Thursday	Donnerstag
Friday	Freitag
Saturday	Samstag, Sonnabend
Sunday	Sonntag

Months	*Die Monate*
January	Januar
February	Februar
March	März
April	April
May	Mai
June	Juni
July	Juli
August	August
September	September
October	Oktober
November	November
December	Dezember

Seasons	*Die Jahreszeiten*
spring	der Frühling, das Frühjahr
summer	der Sommer
autumn	der Herbst
winter	der Winter

Numbers		*Die Zahlen*	
1	eins	5	fünf
2	zwei	6	sechs
3	drei	7	sieben
4	vier	8	acht

9	neun	700	siebenhundert
10	zehn	800	achthundert
11	elf	900	neunhundert
12	zwölf	1000	tausend
13	dreizehn	2000	zweitausend
14	vierzehn	1000000	eine Million
15	fünfzehn	1st	erste(r, s)
16	sechzehn	2nd	zweite(r, s)
17	siebzehn	3rd	dritte(r, s)
18	achtzehn	4th	vierte(r, s)
19	neunzehn	5th	fünfte(r, s)
20	zwanzig	6th	sechste(r, s)
21	einundzwanzig	7th	siebte(r, s)
22	zweiundzwanzig	8th	achte(r, s)
23	dreiundzwanzig	9th	neunte(r, s)
24	vierundzwanzig	10th	zehnte(r, s)
25	fünfundzwanzig	11th	elfte(r, s)
26	sechsundzwanzig	12th	zwölfte(r, s)
27	siebenundzwanzig	13th	dreizehnte(r, s)
28	achtundzwanzig	14th	vierzehnte(r, s)
29	neunundzwanzig	15th	fünfzehnte(r, s)
30	dreißig	16th	sechzehnte(r, s)
40	vierzig	17th	siebzehnte(r, s)
50	fünfzig	18th	achtzehnte(r, s)
60	sechzig	19th	neunzehnte(r, s)
70	siebzig	20th	zwanzigste(r, s)
80	achtzig	21st	einundzwanzigste(r, s)
90	neunzig	30th	dreißigste(r, s)
100	hundert	31st	einunddreißigste(r, s)
200	zweihundert	40th	vierzigste(r, s)
300	dreihundert	50th	fünfzigste(r, s)
400	vierhundert	60th	sechzigste(r, s)
500	fünfhundert	70th	siebzigste(r, s)
600	sechshundert	80th	achtzigste(r, s)

90th	neunzigste(r, s)	800th	achthundertste(r, s)
100th	hundertste(r, s)	900th	neunhundertste(r, s)
200th	zweihundertste(r, s)	1000th	tausendste(r, s)
300th	dreihundertste(r, s)	2000th	zweitausendste(r, s)
400th	vierhundertste(r, s)	millionth	millionste(r, s)
500th	fünfhundertste(r, s)	two millionth	
600th	sechshundertste(r, s)		zweimillionste(r, s)
700th	siebenhundertste(r, s)		

Proverbs and idioms *Sprichwörter und Idiome*

to be homesick — Heimweh haben

I have pins and needles in my foot — mir ist der Fuß
eingeschlafen

it's none of your business — es geht dich (Sie) nichts
an

it's all the same to me — das ist mir egal

as deaf as a post — völlig taub

to sleep like a log — schlafen wie ein Murmeltier

as drunk as a lord — stockbesoffen

a bird in the hand is worth two in the bush — lieber der
Spatz in der Hand als die Taube auf dem Dach

to kill two birds with one stone — zwei Fliegen mit
einer Klappe schlagen

at full speed — mit voller Geschwindigkeit

no sooner said than done — gesagt, getan

birds of a feather flock together — gleich und gleich
gesellt sich gern

every cloud has a silver lining — es gibt immer einen
Morgen

a chip off the old block — der Apfel fällt nicht weit
vom Stamm

out of sight, out of mind — aus dem Auge, aus dem
Sinn

practice makes perfect — Übung macht den Meister

many hands make light work — viele Hände machen
  kurze Müh
better late than never — besser spät als nie
at first sight — auf den ersten Blick
in the short term — kurzfristig
in the long run — langfristig
on the other hand — andererseits
in my opinion — meiner Meinung
in fact — in der Tat
in other words — mit anderen Worten

First names	*Vornamen*
Alexander	Alexander
Andrew	Andreas
Anthony	Anton
Bernard	Bernhard
Charles	Karl
Christopher	Christoph
Edward	Eduard
Francis	Franz
George	Georg
Henry	Heinrich
James	Jakob
John	Johann, Hans
Joseph	Joseph
Lawrence	Laurenz
Louis	Ludwig
Martin	Martin
Michael	Michael
Nicholas	Niklas
Paul	Paul
Peter	Peter
Philip	Philip
Raymond	Raimund

Thomas	Thomas
Vincent	Vinzenz
Alice	Alice
Anne	Anna
Catherine	Katharina
Charlotte	Charlotte
Deborah	Deborah
Eleanor	Leonore
Elizabeth	Elisabeth
Ellen	Ellen
Emily	Emilie
Esther	Esther
Frances	Franzisca
Josephine	Josefine
Louise	Luise
Margaret	Margarete
Mary	Maria
Matilda	Mathilde
Ophelia	Ophelia
Patricia	Patricia
Pauline	Paula
Rachel	Rachel
Rose	Rosa
Susan	Susanne
Sylvia	Sylvia
Veronica	Veronika

Signs of the Zodiac	*Die Tierkreiszeichen*
Aquarius	der Wassermann
Pisces	die Fische
Aries	der Widder
Taurus	der Stier
Gemini	die Zwillinge
Cancer	der Krebs

Leo	der Löwe
Virgo	die Jungfrau
Libra	die Wage
Scorpio	der Scorpion
Sagittarius	der Schütze
Capricorn	der Steinbock

Prepositions, adverbs and conjunctions
Präpositionen, Adverben und Konjunktionen

against	gegen
at	bei
between	zwischen
for	für
from	von
in	in
of	von
on	auf
to	zu
with	mit
without	ohne
above	oben
down	unten
under	unter
in front of	vor
opposite	gegenüber
forward	vorwärts
behind	dahinter
backwards	rückwärts
close to	nahe bei
near	nahe
far from	weit von
before	vor
after	nach
here	hier

there	da, dort
inside	innen
within	darin
outside	außen
where	wo (place). wohin (direction)
during	während
except	außer
towards	auf… zu
until	bis
according to	gemäß
now	nun, jetzt
often	oft
then	dann
never	nie
always	immer
at once	sofort
soon	bald
still	noch
already	schon
like	wie
how	wie
neither… nor	weder… noch
why	warum
because	weil
if	falls
yes	ja
no	nein
well	gut
badly	schlecht
quickly	schnell
slowly	langsam
enough	genug
when	wann
too	auch

more	mehr
less	weniger
much	mehr
nothing	nichts
nobody	niemand
never	nie
perhaps	vielleicht
once	einmal
instead of	anstatt
often	oft
at times	manchmal